There's a War on You Know!

Rick's Childhood Days of Bliss

Richard Hynes

First Published 2009 by Countyvise Limited,
14 Appin Road, Birkenhead, Wirral CH41 9HH.

British Library Cataloguing in Publication Data.
A catalogue record for this book is available from the British Library.

ISBN 978 1 906823 13 9

I would like to dedicate this short memory of the war to all the mothers and women, who despite not having their men around, rationing and shortages, with true grit and determination made an excellent job of looking after their children so well, and also to my own children for prompting me to write about my life as a child in those times. As for me, I loved it, it was my boyhood, and there was a war going on you know.

FIRST DAY AT SCHOOL

NORRIS GREEN 1937

I'm going to school today, my name is Richard and I'm five years old, my Mam is taking me. "Come here son, lets see behind your ears. I don't want you going to school with spuds growing out of them. Good lad, nice and clean, now slick your hair down, you've got a cows lick." I put my hand under the tap and wet my hair with some corporation hair oil, as we kids call the tap water. Now we're off, Monksdown Road council school here I come. I'm excited, the school classes began a few weeks ago, but I could not start until I was five. I've just met Miss Morris, she's one of the headmistresses and she's taking me to my class. I see my Mam looking through the window and mouthing, "You behave yourself." I'm sitting next to a boy, his name is Baker, he never gets called by any other name. All day Miss says "Baker stop that" or "Baker do this". After a little while Baker says to me, "Why don't you be naughty?" "Why?' I ask. "You have to sit on the mat, and you can see Miss Cork's knickers." "I don't want to be naughty, I'd rather sit here by the nature table." Anything about nature I love, much better, I thought, than seeing the teacher's bloomers.

My Mam doesn't come to collect me at four o'clock, so I go home with my elder brother. He's in a hurry and he runs off, I walk home on my own. I take my time, throwing stones, kicking tin cans, other lads chase after me, just because I don't live in their street and they don't know me, they want to beat me up. I go home the longer way, I'm home an hour late. My loving, caring mother of the morning now wants to kill me, she was worried about me, so she now wants to kill me. My Dad's answer to everything was "Give me my belt Mrs, I'll sort it out." Dodging around the table, it was an oval shape, I wonder if it started off square, and the corners have worn away with me running around them. "Stand still while I belt you" was his cry. "No thanks" I'd think, and out of the back door I would run and hide until he cooled down.

Now that I go to school my Mam and Dad let me play out a lot more. Opposite our house there is a swing park, and inside there are lots of things to play on. There's a maypole and a monkey ladder, lots of swings and two saddles, these are what I like best. They are made of big heavy pieces of wood and iron, in the middle are pieces of iron, these we hold on to so that we don't fall off as the saddle is moved back and forward by two lads, one standing on each end.They stand up and by holding two iron bars and then bending their legs at the knees they straighten them again, which moves the saddle. It gets higher and higher, it goes over the beam which is a safety mark.

One lad was playing paratroopers, he jumped off the end then turned to shout how far he'd landed. Then at a terrible speed the saddle swung back and hit him full in the mouth, he lost most of his teeth and broke his nose. No sooner was he out of hospital, when someone pushed a house brick off the building in the bowling green and it landed on his head, he was never the same lad again, I think he was scared to play out.

Alongside the swings there is a lovely bowling green. Children are not allowed in on their own, so we sneak through the bushes and watch the men playing bowls, and dream of the day when we can wear longies and be allowed to play.

At the end of Muirhead Avenue East there are some country cottages, lots of the people who live in them sell flowers, the gardens are full of colour. Mr Addy's garden is on the end. Old Addy, as he gets called, has a field at the bottom of his garden, there are trees near the wall. One of the older boys climbs a tree and ties a rope on a branch then on to the other end a stick is tied, this is to sit on. Each lad takes a turn of climbing onto the wall, then swinging out and back on to the wall again. This is great fun until Old Addy spots us, he runs from his cottage then wacks out at you with a big stick, if he catches you it stings. After a few days he gets a ladder and cuts the rope down, the next day somebody is missing a rope either from a cart or a wagon, and the swing reappears again.

Last weekend I went with some older lads to a garden fete, it was in a meadow on Lord Sefton's estate, we were supposed to pay at the gate, but some older lads showed me how to get in without paying. Over a wall we climbed, not making a sound so that the gamekeepers wouldn't hear us, creeping through the woods and then crawling through bushes, it was really exciting. After crawling under a barbed wire fence we were in for free, but now they wanted money from us to watch a film, this was being shown in a big tent, so under the tent flaps we crawled.

The film was stupid, it was about a brush and a comb getting married, and in it was a doll called Raggedy Ann. Some lad made us laugh by saying we should ask for our money back.

The ice cream man, who rides a bicycle with an ice box on the front and on the side there's a sign which reads 'Stop me and buy one', we can stop him but we don't have any money to buy one. But today we didn't need any money, the man opened the lid on the ice box and then began throwing everything out on to the street, ice lollies and blocks of ice cream, all the kids were grabbing as many ice lollies as they could carry. He then began loading the ice box with bricks and stones, and jumped on to the bike and began peddling like mad around the Crescent, followed by scores of ice lolly sucking kids all curious to see what he was up to. Suddenly he stopped, then lifting the lid on the ice box, he began throwing stones and bricks at the windows of a house, not stopping until all the front window panes were broken. Someone said that his lady friend had chucked him for someone else. I told my Mam what had happened, she said "I hope her new boyfriend is a glazier, because she's certainly going to need one now."

I'm seven now, and in the last two years we've had two different teachers in our class, older ones, not ones that Baker would want to sit on the mat for. The thing that I have noticed about them, is that they each have a mole on their chin, with a hair growing out of it, then I wonder, do older women teachers need to have these to get their jobs? I like school, I love the nature table and painting pictures. We have a band in class, I can never get anything other than the cymbal. This was because my Mam, says, "Have good manners, let others have first choice." I soon forget about those good manners, then I begin getting a drum. Monksdown, or Monkey as the kids call it, is a nice school, it has a lot of pupils. Norris Green is a new housing estate, built for people from the overcrowded slums of the city.

My Mam says lots of people shared one tap in a whole street, some moved in with their bits of furniture on the back of a coal cart, others pushed handcarts all the way from their old neighbourhood down near the docks. These are mainly young families, so there are lots of children, so many that the infants part of the school is split into two sections, Miss Morris has one section and Miss Willet the other. This splitting up of the kids has led to war, the Morries hate the Willies, and so Willies hate the Morries. On the way home I am often asked, "Hey lad are you a Morrie or a Willie?" Knowing the lads are Willies, I would lie, "I'm a Willie", then when I got a safe distance from them, I would shout, "Hah! Hah! No I'm not a smelly, ugly Willie, I'm a Morrie", only to bump into them again and run like hell or get bashed up.

THE MAD DOG

Since I started school two years ago, I have made a few mates, one of these is a lad called Billy, he lives just around the corner from the school. The house Billy lives in backs on to a house that keep a fierce dog in the garden, and he insists I go home with him to have a chase from this dog. I'm thinking I don't need a mad dog running after me, but decide to go, not wanting Billy to think I'm a coward. When we reach his house at dinnertime, Billy tells me to roll my socks down and follow him. One sock was already down, so rolling the other one down I nervously followed him, over the fence we went, into the neighbour's back garden and stopped by the bin. "There's no dog here", I whispered, feeling a lot better now, and relieved. "Watch this," said Billy, and gave the bin an almighty kick, with that a huge nasty looking dog shot out of the shed. "Run around the bin!" Billy is shouting, "But let it catch you and bite your legs!" I'm running now as fast as my little legs will take me. Suddenly the dog is upon me, I'm waiting for the pain from its bite, it bites and bites again, then I realise, its got no teeth, it's gummy. The more it tries the angrier it gets, its mouth just slides off my legs. Billy and I went back to school that afternoon with the cleanest legs in Liverpool.

A DAY OUT IN NEW BRIGHTON

A few months ago I almost got drowned. My Dad and Mam decided to take me and my two brothers and my sister for a day out. We went to New Brighton, which is across the river, everyone in Liverpool calls it 'over the water'. Mam borrowed a little suitcase from the woman next door to take a few things with us. I was so pleased that day, I had my new little suit on. After a ride on the tram to the Pier Head, we boarded the ferry and sailed to New Brighton Pier. When we docked, my elder brother James and I were so excited we ran on ahead, off the pier and on to the sands we ran, waiting for the rest to catch up. "Don't go away too far you two, d'yer hear", in his grumpy voice, he was never keen on days out my Dad. Jimmy and myself decided to go to the boating lake, we walked around to the far side, my brother was talking to another lad. I noticed that over on the other side of the boating lake some kids and their Mams were paddling, must be a little too deep here, I thought, so rolling up my new short trousers a little, thinking my Mam will kill me if I get these wet, I stepped into the water. I remember going down and down, waiting forever for my feet to touch the bottom but they never did, then I was clawing at a wall. Then I shot up again, and down, then up, someone grabbed me and pulled me out, it was my elder brother and the lad he was talking to. My fingers and toes were bleeding with clawing at the wall, and I was being sick. My new suit was pulled off me, and put in the case, I was then told to put on my sister's knickers and my brother's mackintosh. The ferry was packed going home and someone stole the suitcase, and not only had my new suit gone, but also the neighbour's case. My Mam never really wanted to borrow Mrs Dirken's case, she is always moaning, now she will have a great moan. My Mam will still have to pay the tallyman every Saturday morning until the suit is paid for, and Mrs. Dirken will want a new suitcase. Needless to say my Dad never took us on any more days out. With the words from my Dad, "Never again Mrs," we made our way home on the tram.

WAR BREAKS OUT

Mam and Dad went mad the other day, my younger brother Gerard found my Mam's purse and put her money down a slot in the window ledge. It took my Dad all afternoon to take loads of bricks from out of the wall to reach the money and a lot longer to put them back. My Dad has managed to get a few weeks' work as a hod carrier for McAlpines, the builders. I'm helping my Mam to make his butties, his carry out as my Mam calls them. I like the way she makes his brew, she gets a piece of the Echo, and on the newspaper she spoons together dry tea and sugar, then makes a hole in the middle, into this she drops a blob of connie onnie, this is condensed milk, I like connie onnie on a buttie myself, she then folds it up. When my Dad has a brew in work he tosses the lot, newspaper and all, into his billy can and fills it with hot water.

I'm sitting on the front step of our house, it's a Sunday morning. A man is coming through the opening over the road and he's shouting, "Echo! Echo! Read all about it! War declared!" He carries a board with just one word on it - WAR. I'm about to go fishing with my net, I can't play in our back any more. We had a little tent our Uncle Peter and Auntie Mollie gave us, and some water pistols. My brother was chasing me with his water pistol, I was the Baddie as usual and he was the Goodie. We had great fun until the Goodie tripped over a tent rope, he went in the ambulance to hospital with a tent peg still through his cheek. My Dad has taken the tent down and he's hidden the water pistols. Suddenly everybody is out in the street, the women being the most excited, "Will your feller be going Alice?" said Mrs Brown. "No chance, worse luck," replied Alice, "He's on the docks, they don't have to go, I'll never get shut of him." "Where are they going Mam"? I ask. "They're joining up son, in the army or the navy, whoever wants them", said my Mam. "Why Mam?" "To fight the Germans," she replied. I don't even know who the Germans are - oh yes I do, my Dad fought them when he was young. He called them the Jerries, or square heads. One of his brothers was killed, he would have been our Uncle Jimmy.

DAD JOINS UP

A few days later and my Dad has joined up, as everybody called it. He is now in the Royal Air Force, my Mam says we will have some steady money coming in to the house with her allowance from the Royal Air Force. My Dad, like most men, has been finding it hard getting work, mostly on building sites. If it rains you're rained off, so there are no wages. Sometimes he would go to the docks, then stand in a thing called the Pen and if you didn't get picked out by the man in charge, you didn't get any work. My Dad says he picks his cronies from the ones that buy him his ale in the pub. My Dad was in the last war, he was seventeen years old in The Lancashire Fusiliers, which he said was the Great War in 1914-1918. Now it is the year 1939 and he's in again, but this time as an airman. He's gone away now to do his training, but he hasn't gone far, just a few miles up the road to a place called Fazakerly. There's a few weeks gone by now, my Dad like most men from around here have now gone away, mostly in the Army, but some in the Navy and Air Force.

We've had a warning from my Mam, "Behave yourselves, I can smack harder than your Dad and I don't need a belt to do it." I can believe that, as my Mam has arms like tree trunks; I think it is with turning the handle on the mangle in the yard, when she does the washing. Sometimes I try to turn it with two hands and it doesn't move, and there's no washing in it.

THE AIR RAID SHELTER

Lots of things have been happening lately. Two men came to the house and dug a hole in the back garden, then they put together a number of steel sheets by using nuts and bolts, which then formed an arch. They have stuck this in the hole, it has a gap in the front so that we can crawl in and out. It's called an Anderson air raid shelter. The men then told my brother and I to cover it over with soil as they haven't the time, they have loads to do. This we are told is our air raid shelter for if or when we get bombed. Looking at it I hope the Germans only have little bombs. I went into it today and it's muddy. It hasn't even rained yet and there is a few inches of water inside. My Mam reckons we'll all be drowned before the bombs come, if we go in there. In school we're putting strips of sticky brown paper on the window panes, this we are told is to stop the glass from shattering

if a bomb drops nearby. Does this mean perhaps if I put sticky paper all over me I wont shatter? Not much use if it drops on us I thought. There are men building brick air raid shelters almost everywhere, even in the school yard.

PREPARING FOR THE AIR RAIDS.

Down town my Mam says the soldiers are putting sandbags outside the entrances of big buildings, these are to try and stop the blast from the bombs that are coming. We've been given gas masks, they are in a cardboard box. They are made with rubber and have a metal nose piece and a celluloid eye piece to look through, when you put it on it stinks, a lot like the rubber mask the dentist in the clinic puts on your face. It's November now and it's getting dark earlier in the evenings, everybody has been told to put heavy dark curtains on their windows, not a chink of light must shine out. There is an official blackout now, and any person not doing this will be in trouble, no lights must be seen as this will help the German bombers. Some people haven't got a penny for the meter anyway, so they light a candle. My Mam, like many other women, has managed to get hold of some flour sacks. She has taken the stitching out of them and made curtains, she then dyed them black. It's really dark outside on the streets, there's no street lighting and cars and trams drive with dimmed lights. When we go out to play we have to call really loud to find our mates, ours is a call like Tarzan, which we repeat until we meet up with whoever is playing out. Big barrage balloons are appearing in the skies, these are filled with gas and are attached to steel cables. I'm told that they are to try to stop any German bombers hoping that they will fly into the cables. Sometimes lightning strikes the cables and set the balloons on fire. There are big guns on Carr Lane field, they are called Ack Ack guns. They are waiting for any enemy aircraft that come over, and they are manned by soldiers.

THE GAMEKEEPERS

Myself and the rest of our little gang are still going down Crocky to play, as we call Croxteth Hall Estate. We walk past the big Hall, this is where Lord and Lady Sefton live, they have lots of servants, and gardeners and staff to run everything for them. Then we walk across a small bridge, this takes us over the River Alt, in the summer time we paddle in the Alt. Sometimes in the late summer we have eaten apples that the current bring along, floating down the river, having fallen from some tree somewhere along the river bank. The lane we walk along is public so we don't need to keep our eyes open for any of the gamekeepers, we are not on friendly terms with them anyway They don't like us going into the woods after conkers or fishing, and they also think we want to collect pheasant eggs in the spring. If we see any we don't walk past them, after all they only want to protect them so that they and Lord Sefton's friends can shoot them when they have hatched and are grown up. All we want them for is our Mams, they can use them in their cooking. We lads think the gamekeepers should be in the army anyway, shooting enemy soldiers instead of little pheasants who can't shoot back.

THE ARMY CAMP

We reach our goal which is the army camp, it has been built in part of the woods on the Croxteth Estate. The lane that runs past Lord Sefton's house runs through the centre of the camp and on the left, in a small field, stands the cookhouse. The soldiers who are the cooks give us loads of cakes to eat, they have invited all of us back in a few weeks time for our Christmas dinner, three cheers for the British army. We can't wait for Christmas now, we are all so excited. I've told my younger brother he can come, I think every other lad has told his brother also. Our little gang seems to be a much bigger gang now as the news spreads. As Christmas nears I'm really looking forward to it, we've been down Crocky and collected lots of holly, this we have hung around pictures that are on the walls of our house. Paper chains for decorations are made from coloured paper, we're sticking them together with paste made from flour and water. "We'll be looking for that flour to make bread with, my lad, the way things are going," says my Mam.

Christmas Day has arrived at long last, and Father Christmas has been, he's left us an apple and an orange and some sweets. They're in a sock which hangs from the fireplace, we each have a sock. A boy in class told me there's no Father Christmas, it's your Dad. It can't be our Dad, he's away in the forces I told him. My Mam said, "Father Christmas can't bring any toys, because there is a war on, and the Germans have got them all." He didn't get them all though, my mate, the one whose Dad is a docker, got a train set and a farm. Funny thing is, each boy that I know whose Dad is a docker seemed to get loads for Christmas. Anyway it's the army camp for our Christmas dinner, and we can't wait. We get a wash from my Mam, she wont let us wash ourselves, because we will only give ourselves a cats lick as she calls it, so she washes behind our ears and around our necks. "I don't want you two making a show of me, with tide marks around your necks," she says. Then at long last we're on our way to the army camp, making good time by running along and shouting, "Last one there gets nothing and his Dad is a Nazi!" We are all welcomed by the soldiers and they are looking after us well. There's lots to eat, turkey and chicken, lots of pudding, custard with rum in it, which we think tastes horrible. Some soldiers are drunk and are throwing lots of ciggies around, some kids are collecting them to take home for their big sisters to smoke, and to have a sly whiff themselves. My younger brother Gerard ran all the way home with a turkey for my Mam, it's only had a few slices cut off it, it's nearly as big as him. My Mam will be well pleased with that, he's run all the way back now to join in the fun. We are home now, all of us well fed, my Mam say's to make the most of it, as most things are going to be rationed shortly.

THE SATURDAY CRUSH

Every Saturday afternoon we go to the pictures, the Saturday matinee or the Saturday crush, this is at the West Derby cinema, which is known locally as the Wezzy. Some kids call it the flea pit, and say that they go there for a laugh and a scratch. It costs three pence to get in, if you're a posh kid you pay four pence. We're from the Corpy houses, so we go in the three pennies. Each lad has his own way of getting his entrance money, it is done in many ways. Some lads have paper rounds or run messages, sometimes we climb along the wall at the back of the shops, until we reach the yard of The Chocolate Box, that's our local sweet shop, then reach down and get a few empty lemonade bottles which are stacked in the yard. Then we take them around to the shop front, not altogether but at intervals, and get the deposit from the bottles. Sometimes if we find any boxwood, it's chopped up into sticks, then with some wire we make bundles of firewood. The chandlers shop will always buy it, but it's better if you sell it around the houses, we get more money for it.

THE MILK ROUND

I help Old Daddy Harper on his milk round. Harper's dairy farm is on the corner of Hornspit Lane and Almonds Green. They have two milk rounds and each one has a horse to pull the milk float, one horse is named Peggy and the other is Polly. I help before I go to school, also on Saturday and Sunday. He gives me a sixpence for my wages each Saturday morning, but I have to confess, when he goes into the house for his porridge and a piece of cheese I take another sixpence out of his money bag, which he hangs up in the milk house. I thought sixpence wasn't much for seven mornings a week, then I dread going to confession. Going on the milk round in the winter is freezing cold. The milk is in a big metal churn on the float, this is the cart. I have to take the top off the churn then scoop the milk out into a can with a handle on it, then pour it into jugs that people have left on the step. Some jugs have narrow tops and you're scared to spill any of the milk. Some also have fancy lace covers over the top. At one house I deliver to at the weekend, each time I walk up the big driveway to the door a big fat lad stands at the window, from the warmth and comfort of his house and sticks his tongue out at me. I shake my fist at him and vow to meet him some day and get my own back. I look each Saturday afternoon to see if he comes out of the fourpennies in the Wezzy picture house so that I can give him a fourpenny one on his fat nose, but it never happens.

Peggy and Polly, the horses, know every house to stop at that give them a crust of bread, they also walk on along the streets then stop at each house that has milk delivered without being told to. This I think is really clever of them. A small elderly man who wears a long black overcoat and has a huge cap, big enough to carry ten pounds of spuds in as my Mam would say, helps on the milk; Old Jonesey he's called. He's a Welshman, crafty Taffy I call him. He and Mr Harper know every house that gives a tip or a bar of chocolate on payday, each one telling me, "Alright son I'll do that house". It's not only the horses that seem to know the best houses to call at.

THE LOCAL PICTURES

The Wezzy picture house, the West Derby Cinema, is a magical place, it's in West Derby village. The doorman, who also is the fireman, has a big bushy moustache, and wears a uniform like he's The Admiral Of The Fleet. It has gold braid hanging from the shoulders of the jacket, my Mam would say that he's done up like a dog's dinner, and he also has a big red face like a farmers bum on a frosty morning, another of my Mam's sayings. He carries around with him a big stick and often belts us with it as we wait in the queue. It's only lads like myself who are in the threepenny queue who get belted, never the posh kids in the fourpennies, maybe they behave themselves much better than we corporation house kids. The manager's name is Mr Percival Tonge, the kids call him Percy the Penguin, but that's behind his back. He always wears a black dress suit plus a dicky bow and looks like a penguin. Every Saturday without fail he stops the film and amid the shouts of 'put a penny in the leccy', he threatens to keep the film off until everyone in the pictures behave themselves. Then as soon as he gets some order and the film starts again, so does the throwing of the apple cores and orange peel, most of it landing on the posh kids. When my Mam is annoyed she always says, "I'll give you a fourpenny one in a minute my lad," maybe that's where her saying came from, us kids throwing at the fourpenny ones. We have a serial to watch each Saturday, sometimes it's Flash Gordon. He's usually fighting the Claymen, or it could be The Clutching Hand. Lots of kids get a bit scared of that, especially the girls, so we have found that if we get a chicken leg from the butcher's bin and pull the tendons the claw opens and closes, these are great when the Clutching Hand is on. The girls are terrified when we sit behind them with our own made clutching hands. We lads aren't scared of anything though, except our Mams and the game keepers, or the ghost of the monk down Meadow Lane. But it's mostly the Cowboy and Indian films that we like best, we seem to get home a lot quicker, smacking our bottoms and pretending we are riding our horses, a black horse for a baddy, the goody always rides a white horse.

OUR IGLOO

Winter is almost over now, and it's staying lighter, it isn't going dark until pretty late and there hasn't been a bombing raid yet.

There was a heavy fall of snow a few weeks back, the snow swept over the fences. I was battered by my Mam, she sent me across the road to borrow a night light from a neighbour, the snow had drifted over the fence and I was trying to find the fence to climb over when I fell and dropped the night light. With it being so small and white, and because it was also a dark night, I had no chance of finding it in the snow. When I told my Mam she gave me a good smacking. I think she was so fed up, we had no light. My Mam's nerves had gone, I think she smacked me more because I never would cry.

The snow was so deep the trams stopped running. Us lads had a great time, we got our money for the pictures by clearing people's paths of snow. These were mainly in the posh houses, the same houses that we go to when carol singing at Christmas. It is always a waste of time carol singing around were we live because nobody ever has any money. Our little gang made an igloo, we built it around the lamp post. The grocer Mister Cassidy gave us a big square biscuit tin, I was surprised he gave it to us after the loads of cheek we give him, such as shouting into his shop, "Have you any empty boxes, well fill them", or "Have you any broken biscuits, well mend them". We made snow pies with the biscuit tin, much the same as making sand pies, these were used to build the walls. Planks of wood borrowed from here and there made the roof. Snow was piled over the top and a hole was cut in the side for getting in and out of the igloo. It froze that night and our gang had a great den, it was there for ages. Let Adolf try and bomb us now, I thought.

DOYLES CAFÉ

My Mam has started working, it's at my Auntie Louise's café. It's also a chip shop, and it's near the docks, just around the corner from the Gordon Smith Institute where lots of merchant seamen stay when on shore, and wait for their next ship. Also the Sailors' Home is opposite, so the café is busy all day. Mam takes my young sister with her, she's too young for school. My Uncle Pat usually works in the café, but he's away with the Eighth Army fighting in the desert. The café is called Doyles after my Uncle Pat Doyle, my Mam's brother. Mam made us swear not to mention that she is working to my Dad when he comes home on leave. He's old fashioned, my Mam says, and wouldn't like the idea of my Mam working.

I go now and again to see my Mam at work. The café is in Price Street, it's always full with merchant seamen from all over the world. Sometimes I take my younger brother Gerard with me, we ride on a tram to the Pier Head then walk along the dock road underneath the overhead railway, known by everyone as the dockers' umbrella. It's very busy along the dock road with horses and carts. Huge cart horses, their hooves slipping on the cobbles as they strain to pull big heavy carts, weighed down with loads of goods from the docks. Steam engines run along the road under the overhead railway, a man walking in front waving a red warning flag. There are tramcars, also lorries filled with soldiers, lots of ships on the river, each one either loading or unloading their cargoes and all adding to this mighty sound and the smell, a mixture of spices, peanuts, molasses, brown sugar and even horse muck, all mixing together to make this wonderful sweet yet not unpleasant smell. Since my Mam began work we lads have little jobs to do, one of mine is to collect a can of milk from Harpers each night after school. I don't like doing this, mainly because my enemies, the posh kids, lie in wait. They have their catapults at the ready and they aim at the can, but hit me more often than their target. I swear I'll catch up with them one by one.

NITCHA AND THE OWL

It's well into Spring now, I have a new mate, his nickname is Nitcha. He doesn't have a roof in his mouth so his voice sounds different, but I can understand him. We go looking for birds eggs on Lord Sefton's Estate, without his permission of course, making sure to keep our eyes open for the Gamies, or Gamekeepers as they like to be called. The lads have their own names for them, one is known as The Lash, he has a whip and he doesn't think twice about using it if he catches you on private land. Then there's Plus Fours, he wears big baggy trousers pushed down into his socks, then Jack Flash, who's got no chance of catching us. He's a big fat man, he must be about twenty stone, he's puffing and blowing when he's walking.

We find a lot of eggs and we know the names of the type of bird that laid them. I ask Nitcha if he has ever heard of a Fossilusal bird. He hasn't, so I tell him it's extinct, it used to fly around in ever decreasing circles, until one day it vanished up its own backside. "Is that right, do you know any more?" he asked. There is an Egyptian bird I tell him, and it's got a triangled shaped bum, for sitting on the top of the Pyramids. "Isn't nature wonderful," he said. We blow the eggs by getting a thorn from an hawthorn bush, make a hole in the egg then suck out the yolk. Sometimes the egg is addled, that is a baby bird is forming, then I feel guilty. It doesn't seem to bother Nitcha.

We went to the army camp, and met a lad who told us that he's seen a big owl, and he thinks it's nesting somewhere in the army camp. The camp is empty now, because the soldiers have left. My Mam said that more than likely they went to Dunkirk. We saw Dunkirk on the news at the pictures, lots of soldiers were killed on the beaches. I hope our soldier mates are alright, they were kind to us. After looking at almost every tree we found one with a big hole in. "I bet it's nesting in there," Nitcha whispered. I'm first to climb the tree, because I have pumps on. Putting my hand inside the hole and feeling around, "There's nothing here Nitch," I told him. "Let me try, lend me your pumps, I can't climb with these clogs on" he said, in that voice only his Mam and I can understand. Up he went, he found the nest in another hole much further up the tree. "There's two eggs in it," he shouted. Then the biggest owl I've ever seen flew at him. Nitcha fell out of the tree screaming until he hit the floor still clutching the eggs, he was moaning about his back, but my concern was getting my pumps back, I couldn't run very fast with his clogs on. If anyone is going to get caught it's not going to be me, as I'm sure every gamekeeper on the estate must have heard his screaming.

The miracle was the eggs hadn't broken, but it was all a waste of time. I felt guilty - the eggs were addled. I'm not playing with Nitcha, because with the words "Bombs away" he dropped the eggs off the bridge in Croxteth Hall Lane onto the road below. We have made a collection of eggs using the egg boxes we find in Cassidy the grocer's bin.

TURNIPS AND APPLES

The next day a few of us went looking for frog spawn. We have our jam jars and milk bottles to put the frog's spawn in, the teacher at school wants some for her nature table. Walking home we met some older lads who not only took the frog spawn from us, but also threw some at us. Then despite telling them that his brother was in their class in school and will kill them, they put a load down one of the lads wellies; they made him walk home in his squelchy wellies.

It's well into summer now and people who have been 'Digging for Victory' in their allotments and gardens are now beginning to see their vegetables grow. We also see them and now and again sample a few radish or a lettuce. Our best feed though is to go across Mister Wood's fields and grab a turnip, or as we call them a tonny, knock the roots and soil off on a gate post, then peel it with our teeth. They are nice and juicy and fill you up. If we are out for the day and we have a juicy turnip each, when a farm hand or anybody is approaching along the lane, usually on a bike, the first lad to spot them sings "All away, all away, all away all" and suddenly there's not a turnip in sight, disappearing under jerseys and down trousers in a blink of an eye.

It's August now and the apples are ripe, the orchards are laden down with fruit but still they are scarce in the shops, a shortage of people to pick them so Mrs Malley the greengrocer told my Mam, so us lads decide to help the war effort. We raid Woodsy's, the farmer's orchard, and help ourselves. Mister Woods doesn't take kindly to kids, especially the ones nicking his apples from his orchard, so he keeps a huge male pig. It's a boar and it's vicious, it has big tusks, but fortunately for us it sleeps most of the time in an old tin shed that's falling apart and full of holes. It's in the far corner of the orchard, built against the wall, this is a challenge to us kids, so we play commandos. One lad walks along the wall and peeps through a crack in the roof of the pig shed, if it's asleep he raises his right arm, if not and its awake he runs like mad and we move on. This time we are in luck, he raises his arm and as one we run to the apple trees. We have to be quick and climb into the tree, if the pig wakes up we'll be up there for ages. We have enough so back over the wall and down into the ditch at the side of the lane for the share out. Every one lays their apples on the grass, then each lad takes a turn to pick one until they have all gone. We do this while wearing a blindfold, nobody has a hanky so a piece of old rag is used instead. One lad always keeps out of the apple raids, saying "I'll keep douse, 'cos if I get caught, I'll get expelled from school." He only goes to an ordinary council school like all of us. We have not sat for the scholarship yet, we are too young. When we are old enough he will fail anyway, he's too thick, he's as thick as a railway mug. So when it's his turn to pick, if his hand is over a nice apple we move the apple and replace it with a manky one. The lads think this is justice, because he's a coward.

A few days ago we almost got caught, there was a cry of 'look out here's Woodsy', every lad got away, having reached the safety of some scrub land on the corner of Dwerryhouse Lane and Muirhead Avenue. Nitcha asked, "Where's my coat?" "I don't know," I replied. "I shouted for you to grab it," he said. I can hardly make out what Nitcha says at the best of times, nevermind when Mister Woods and his dogs are chasing us. We looked across from our hiding place in time to see Woodsy pick the coat up and head back to his farm. "Oh! My Mam will batter me, if I go home without my coat," said Nitcha. "You must be joking Nitch, the state of it, the lining is ripped, you stuffed in half of the orchard, you're greedy you kept going back for more," I said. "I can't go home without it," he said, almost crying. "The ragman wouldn't take that old coat Nitch," I said, trying my best to get him to forget about it. But he stayed out late, then plucked up enough courage to knock at the farm house door and ask for his coat back. Mrs Woods, the farmer's wife, gave it back to him, I think she was only glad to, fearing the dogs might catch something from it. Then Nitcha said to me, "The lousy buggers have taken the apples out."

FIRST AIR RAID

We had a proper air raid last night, it was horrible, but exciting as well. The sirens went off a few weeks back, they make a loud wailing and scary noise, but then it was a false alarm, the all clear sounded a short time later. But last night was real, the air raid warden was shouting for everyone to get into their shelters. Me and our Jimmy jumped down into the shelter first, then we helped Gerard our younger brother down, then my Mam with my sister Rose. My Mam said we had better get more organised than this, all we had was a sack over the hole we use to get in and out. We didn't even have a candle so we sat in the dark listening to the drum, drum of the loaded bombers overhead and the sound of the big army guns firing at them, then the bombs exploding. After what seemed a long time everything was quiet and the all clear sounded. "Come on kids, all out, let's go and have some nice hot cocoa," said my Mam. Then one of the neighbours called, her name is Mrs Harrison, or as we call her Old Ma Hags. All of her children are grown up and the five of them are in the forces. I love to hear her talk, after every sentence she says "Anderem". "I got some lovely tripe down the lane Annie, anderem, the knife cut lovely through the seam, anderem. I heard from our Alice the other day, anderem she's stationed down south, anderem. I never hear from the lads, anderem." She's a widow, and my Mam says, "She's lonely without anyone at home, if she wants any messages, run them for her."

RATIONING

Even though there are air raids during the night, we still go to school. If for some reason the school is closed, our class has lessons in Gordon Watson's house which is opposite the school. Food is on ration now and my Mam has her ration books. She's spread them around a bit between Mr Cassidy the grocer, Pegrams a grocers and the Co-op stores. My brother Jimmy and I have to learn the divvy number, it's 185364. We make sure it's given in each time we go on a message, so my Mam will get a dividend sometime, or a divvy as everyone calls it. She also has meat coupons for the butchers, tea, sugar, butter, cheese. It's all rationed now; Mam said we can only get two ounces of tea each week, one ounce of cheese, two ounces fat to cook with, and four ounces of bacon, and two ounces of butter. My Mam said I'll have to stop putting the butter on my bread like a bricklayer. Bread isn't rationed, so we can still enjoy a buttie, a jam one I like best. Mam makes plum jam with some of our sugar ration, or one with connie onny, or black treacle. My young brother, he likes sauce on his. I tell him it's horrible, but he laughs and says "It's O.K." That's not a bad joke from him, because that is the name of the sauce.

THE CHIPPIE

Fish and chips are not rationed. We can't always afford fish so we make do with half a fish cake each. Mam says she doesn't like fish cakes, I think she says this to save the coppers. There are four chippies to pick from. Up the lane there's Rylands, Houghtons, then Cloughs, down the opposite way is Quirks. Mam always sends me to the furthest one which is Cloughs, she thinks you get the most chips from there. I can't kid her and go to one nearer because the chips taste different from each chip shop. On a cold night the lady who serves me gives me the crispy batter that falls from the fried fish, it's nice but the dripping that it's cooked in sticks to the roof of my mouth with the cold. Then I decide to sneak a chip by making a little hole in the newspaper the chips are wrapped in. I pull out a chip, lovely, I'll just have another one, this goes on and on. Nearer home I panic as lots of chips have been eaten and there's now a huge hole in the paper, I unwrap them and try to wrap them like the woman in the chippy, no chance, what a mess. The fish aren't the only things to be battered tonight, my Mam will now batter me. A lad in my class in school, he told me that he ate too many of the chips on the way home so he ate as many as he could, then threw the rest away. When he reached his house he rubbed his eyes until they were red then wet his face and ran in pretending some lads beat him up and took the chips from him. His mother told him, "Never mind son, here's some money, go back again." When he returned he told his Mam he didn't want any as he was too upset to eat, not that he was bursting at the seams with scoffing all the chips.

I spend more time now at Harper's farm. The winter is closing in and it's getting colder, but inside the shippon it's nice and warm. There's lots of cows and their breath helps to keep it warm, also Peggy and Polly the horses are stabled in there, and a massive bull, he's chained away from the cows. Mr Harper tells me that the cows wouldn't have milk but for the bull. Daddy Harper, as I call him, is teaching me how to milk the cows. "Come closer and watch," he says to me. He sits on a little three legged stool a bucket between his legs, and his head pressed against the side of the cow. Come closer, closer, then he squirted a jet of milk all over my face. He thought it was funny, but he did teach me how to milk a cow. "It's squeeze and pull, squeeze and pull," he says. "But I'll give you a tip young man, never try and milk the bull."

He thought this was so funny he almost fell off the milking stool. I helped to muck out and feed the pigs in their sty today. I now have a Swiss army knife, it has lots of blades on it, one of these is called a pig stabber. I got it in exchange, I give a lad a pile of conkers and comics. I keep thinking if the pigs attack me, I'll defend myself with it. I needn't worry, their only interest is the swill and it stinks. Daddy Harper tells me a pig will eat anything, even you lad, if you had more meat on you, the only thing they wont eat are pea pods. Sure enough, at the bottom of their trough there are always pea pods.

In the farm yard stands a big iron pot, and underneath it is a fire. Waste food collected from school kitchens and from swill bins from the milk round is thrown into the pot, it smells really horrible, I now realise why we had gas masks issued. Mrs Harper the farmer's wife, treats me like she's my Granny. I don't mind, I don't have a Granny, if I have I've never seen her. She gives me calendars from Bibby's and Silcock's, who supply cattle food. They have pictures of farmyard animals which I cut out and leave enough underneath to bend and make a stand. I have lots of animals in my toy farm, even a farmer, but the only cockerel I had to cut out was the full page, so I have a cockerel ten times the size of the farmer, it's a sort of King Kong chicken. I heard my Mam telling Mrs Harper that someone told her that she could send us to live in Wales, until the war ends, we would go as evacuees. "No one is taking my kids anywhere," I heard my Mam say. "Bombs or no bombs they stay with me."

MAM'S PRAYERS ARE ANSWERED

We have been getting a lot more air raids lately, we're quite used to them now. Every time a man on a motorbike goes past our house in the night, there is an air raid. We think he has a telephone, and gets told when enemy planes are approaching, then goes to set the sirens off. When we hear the motorbike my

Mam gets the cocoa out and a candle at the ready, and down the smelly shelter we go. A few nights ago the bombs were falling and my Mam would say "Oh a poor dog 'as been hit." "Mam that's the screaming of a bomb." "Oh that's good, the dog's alright then." One night in the shelter there was a sudden hissing noise and a big flash, then the smell of smoke. "Oh Jesus Mary and Joseph have mercy on us, we've been hit, save my babies." "Mam its alright, we're okay, look." We had a tin, a square tin on its side, and my brother Jimmy had put it in the corner. Inside was a lit candle, on the top my mother had put a big box of matches as the heat from the candle hit the tin under the matches they ignited. My Mam's prayers were answered, we were saved.

It's getting near Christmas again, it won't be like the last one. Mam says we may get something from the soldiers and sailors, she said that we are sought of being looked after by a family in Surrey. I think this is because we have nothing, but if your Dad is a docker you're better off, because they have next to nothing. Mr and Mrs Whittaker are the names of the people who are kind to us. Mr. Whittaker is an officer in the Royal Air Force. Mrs Whittaker has been sending letters to my Mam and a few little things to help her along. They have gone to Canada now, Mr Whittaker is stationed there, they have sent us Canadian woollen hats. They're nice but I like my balaclava the best, it keeps my ears warm. It's getting very near Christmas now, the bombers are still coming, the shelter's cold now, Jimmy and myself have got my Mam to stay in the house a few times. Gerard cried a bit, he wanted to go in the shelter. Telling him he can go in by himself he shuts up, and falls asleep. Jimmy and myself sneak upstairs to see any aircraft overhead, there's lots of searchlights across the sky. My brother Jimmy knows lots of planes, German and ours. I'm thrilled when he tells me there's a German plane called a Focker Wulf, I can't wait to say it in front of an adult. When I do, no one seems bothered.

THE HAMPER

Two nights before Christmas and there's a knock on the door, my Mam opens it, and a man and a woman wish her a happy Christmas, then gave her a food hamper. My Mam was delighted, she thanked them, and asked where they came from. They belonged to a mission hall in Muirhead Avenue East, then my Mam had a little weep, at their kindness and us being Catholics. "God love them," she said. Christmas goes by. My Dad comes home on leave. I know when he's home, I hear a deep voice downstairs. He has brought two dead hares home, he shot them on the airfield. We'll have soup from these with barley. He's been home a day and already he has our wireless in bits on the table. "What are you messing with that for Mister," says my Mam. "It's oscillating, Mrs." "Oscillating my a---!" said my Mam, "Put it back together Mister, it's the only bit of enjoyment I get, that and the Daily Mirror." I never hear my Mam or Dad call each other by their names. My Mam is Annie but gets Mrs, my Dad is Dick but gets called Mister. My Dad is going back from leave. "I'm getting off Mrs, back to the safety of the airfield," then he's gone into the blackout. Mam didn't go to work when my Dad was on leave, we were sworn to secrecy not to mention she was working. She's gone back now, it was nice when she was home. When Rose starts school, she will only go to work a few days a week.

THE BULLY

We're back at school. Every morning, because I'm a Catholic and it's a council school, which is church of England, I'm not allowed into assembly. A few of us go into the Catholic room, but I can still hear the lovely hymns coming from the hall. I'm in the juniors now, it's not as nice as the infants. We have mostly men teachers, it's boys only now, the girls have their own part of school. One of the teachers I don't like, his name is Mr Jones.

The kids call him Skyscraper Jones because he is about six foot four. I know he doesn't like me, he bullies me whenever he sees fit. Mr Thomas who is my class teacher picks me to give out school dinners from the trolley in the dining room. My mates like me on the dinners, as they get seconds, especially the syrup tart and custard. But if Mr Jones is on duty at dinner time he tells me to get off. He's not my teacher, but a few times when our teacher leaves the room he looks through the side window and gives me the cane. Even though all the class are making a noise he picks me out and canes me. I told my Mam, she says I must have been doing something wrong. He goes on to my list of people I'll get my own back on when I grow up. I didn't have to wait long, I went to the lavatory the other afternoon and on my way back to class I saw him taking his class for PT in the yard. He had a pair of pumps on his feet. I sneaked into the cloakroom, it wasn't hard to pick out a pair of size twelve shoes. I took great delight in dropping them into the fire bucket the one with water in it. I spent the rest of the lessons in fear, expecting to be called out, but got away with it. Ah well, it's confession again at the weekend. "Forgive me Father, for I have sinned. I dropped Mr Jones' shoes into the fire bucket, I thought they were incendiary bombs." "Is that the bully of a teacher, who is a Protestant?" "Yes Father." "Well that's okay my child, you are forgiven."

TWO PENNY MIXED

Lots of things are on ration now, but not sweets yet. I remember when I was five a big lad called John Tilly and his sister sent me to a neighbour's house. Go and ask Mrs Dirken for the lend of two pennies, tell her your Mam sent you, they're for the gas. They took the money and bought two lollypops, they had one each. I was sitting in the gutter one on each side of me licking away when I was hauled away by the ear. It was my Mam, Mrs Dirken had been watching. She knew what the money was for, and right away told my Mam. "Wicked bitch" is all my Mam said, after giving her the two pennies back. There are two houses in our road that sell sweets, Mr Harwood and next door old Daddy Blanchard. They sell them from a table in the kitchen, me and my mates go to Blanchards for a two penny mixed, this is a Pegs bar and some sweets. I ask my Mam if she has any money, two pence for sweets but give me a tanner, I'll bring the change. "You better had, my lad," says my Mam. The reason I want the sixpence is when old Blanchard goes in the front room for change, we nick a few extra sweets. It's confession once again.

LAY ME AN EGG FOR MY TEA

Apples are now scarce, they're out of season. We buy a pennorth of fades from Malleys, and these are rotten apples with the badness cut out of them. I spend lots of time between Harper's farm and going down Croxteth Estate. If its rainy I go to the farm, I have lots of places to go, in the barn or the shippon, or the loft, I can hide among the bales of hay. Last week I found some eggs, my Mam was well pleased with them. Some hens lay quite a lot in the hay, there's gaps in between the bales, some are near the roof. A few hens hop up and up, and lay their eggs in these gaps. I decide to get more hens laying their eggs in there. The chicken shed has a big lock on it, but it is near the hay loft. and both are well away from the farmhouse. At weekends or school holidays, I also get sent home now and again from school if there's been a long air raid the night before, then I go to the farm. I put a piece of wood against the little hole the chickens use to get into the shed. They can't get in now so they lay in between the bales of hay, more eggs for my Mam. I make sure I take the wood away before I leave. I feel that I have helped the war effort as well as my Mam. The song on the radio is *Hey Little Hen, When, When, When, Will You Lay Me An Egg For My Tea.*

SCARLET FEVER STRIKES

My sister Rose has been ill with scarlet fever. My Mam didn't want to send her to hospital. Her eldest daughter Marie, our sister, died in hospital with diphtheria, she was only six, and my Mam still curses the doctor, he said she only had a cold. Mam did not want to send our sister Rose to hospital so we all caught scarlet fever, Rose, Jimmy, Gerard and myself. It was horrible, my Mam asked a neighbour Mr. Terry to bring a bed down stairs, then nursed all of us. We had nightmares, I could see lions and tigers coming out of the fire. Before he went in the forces, my Dad sent me and my brothers to the top of the stairs with a lit candle. You had to blow the candle out and shout 'Tiger! Tiger!', then walk down the stairs, not run. "What are you making them do that for Mr?" my Mam would ask. "I'm making young men out of them Mrs, you don't want them growing up cissies do you?" "No, but they are not likely to meet a tiger in Norris Green, are they Mister." said my Mam. Now I have been seeing lions as well as tigers. My Mam has had a bad time nursing all of us, the bed is still downstairs.

THE ROCKING CHAIR

One night we had a raid, Jimmy and myself coaxed my Mam to stay in the house. Gerard had a moan, he wanted to go into the shelter. After telling him he can go in by himself, just him and the great big spiders and earwigs that live in there, he soon shut up. The air raid started, it was a bad one. Jimmy and myself began to put the furniture around the bed, much like making a circle out of the cowboy wagons when the Red Indians attacked. We'd seen this on the Saturday matinee. Next we put the two youngest under the bed. My elder brother told my Mam to crawl under the bed, this she did, but being a bit plump, she got stuck with just her bottom sticking out. Being boy scouts we used our scouse nouse and turned the rocking chair upside down, and placed it over my Mam's bottom, now she was safe from the bombs. The raid went on for hours, when the all clear sounded it took us longer to pull my Mam out from under the bed than it did pushing her under it. We lads now collect shrapnel, pieces of bombs and shells that have exploded. We have some shiny pieces and lots of shapes, we do swops. My Mam wont have it in the house, she says, it might have killed someone. All of us kids could go to live in Wales, away from the bombing, it's called evacuation, it's in the countryside. Someone tries again and tells my Mam that we could live on a farm, I'd love to go but my Mam says no one takes her kids away so forget about it. If we get bombed we'll all get bombed together.

MY LOVELY POND

It's now into spring again, and I love it, despite warnings of Jerry aeroplanes might machine gun you. I set off down Crocky Hall Lane by myself, I can see more of nature that way. I have a few favourite places, one is along the lane. A stream runs from Woodsy's field under the lane and comes out in the woods. I climb onto the wall, and if I keep still and quiet I see lots of birds and small animals drinking from the stream. Another of my favourite places is past the gamekeeper's lodge, the one who keeps the hounds in a paddock, he's the one we call Plus Fours. I climb over a stile then through the fence into a large meadow, creeping as close to the ground so I'm out of sight of the farm house, and there it is a lovely big pond. I stretch out on the grass and watch the coots and water hens and lots of ducks. There are water lilies, reeds and loads of bright coloured dragonflies. I spend lots of time here, I'm keeping it a secret, it's my special place. Not even Nitcha knows about my secret speck. Walking home one afternoon along the lane opposite Croxteth Hall a huge badger crossed in front of me, he stopped looked at me as if to say who are you, then just ambled away into the woods. I was amazed, nobody believed me when I told them, they only come out at night like the German bombers I was told. This one must have been working the day shift, I thought.

THREE BLIND KIDS

Sometimes I can't seem to do things right, you know you do something, then it turns out all wrong. Yesterday I was reading a comic, in it is Lord Snooty and friends. He was sitting around the table with his friends. Suddenly, he, that is Lord Snooty, had an idea for a jolly good wheeze, he means having a laugh. Filling his hand with pepper, he blew it at his friends, they were all sneezing and laughing and the boys and girls in the comic thought it was all very jolly. Last night I could hardly wait for our dinner, when my brothers and my sister sat down. I filled my hand with pepper, then I blew. They didn't laugh, they all screamed in pain, tears streaming from their eyes, I had blinded them all. Then with the words, "You evil little bastard," my Mam flew at me. I dodged her and skipped over the fences and away, I stayed out for hours. On the promise that my Mam wouldn't hit me I crept in. She battered me.

MAM'S WORK IS NEVER ENDING

My Mam works very hard, she works all day in the café; when she comes home she cooks for us kids, and then she'll be darning socks or sewing things. At weekends she scrubs out, on her knees she washes the floor with Aunt Sally, not a real Aunty, it's a liquid soap, that's its name. Sometimes I forget and walk across the wet floor. "Mam, can I have a jam buttie?" With the words "I'll give you a jam buttie", the wet floor cloth gets thrown. She never misses, it wraps around my neck. "Mam that's not a jam buttie." "Oh, go and get it, you're a hard faced one." "Thanks Mam can I have the crust?" "Just hurry before I brain you. Child from hell." Mam also does the washing, she has a dolly tub and a set of dolly pegs. She scrubs and bashes the clothes with the dolly pegs, then she puts them through the mangle in the yard, this squeezes the water out. Sometimes she asks me to turn the handle, I try with two hands. "Get away you're useless," she says, then turns the handle with one hand, while steering the sheets in with the other.

Saturday night she bakes, I love when she bakes, she makes jam tarts and custard tarts, scones and more tarts, such as gooseberry or blackcurrant, anything she can get hold of. We fight each other over who scrapes the mixing bowl out. When my Mam is making the pastry I watch, she kneeds the dough and rolls it out on a board sprinkling flour so it doesn't stick. She doesn't have a rolling pin so she uses a milk bottle. Then when it's flat she gets a tea cup, turns it upside down and stamps it out into circles, these she places in the baking tray. Then she puts the filling in, and then it goes into the oven. The best to watch is when she makes the big pies on a dinner plate, a large slice of pastry goes on the plate, then apple with sugar, pastry goes over the top, she then puts the plate on one hand and then cuts around the edge with a knife. After making a few of these we have the dough that's left to make little pastry men, these go into the oven with currants for eyes. We get one jelly a week because its rationed. I asked why one jelly a week and was told it's made from gelatine and its also used to make bombs. I don't know if this is true, I cant imagine big bombs of jelly being dropped on the Germans, maybe she means gelignite. Mam puts it in a bowl then pours boiling water on it, she stirs it around until it all dissolves, then puts it on the kitchen window ledge to set. Sometimes I sneak out and drink half of it, then top it back up with cold water. Sunday morning I hear my Mam calling old Mr Cassidy everything. "I don't know what kind of a jelly he gave me, it's like maiden's water, it won't set. He'll set when I see him, I'm taking my ration book out of there."

PEA PICKING

The war still goes on, everybody sees lots of the war on the pictures, it's on Pathe News. A big cheer goes up when our soldiers are on, and a boo when the German soldiers are on. To get a few coppers we decide to go pea picking. We are on our school holidays, usually we go for free dinners to a wooden building in Strawberry Road, which is in Broadway. Even though we are tempted by the rice pudding with a dollop of jam in the middle, my mates and I decide not to go to the dinner centre and instead we thumb a lift from a wagon or lorry driver to take us along the East Lancashire Road. There are lots of farms, and we manage to get pea picking jobs right away. I told my Mam I'll make loads of money. Me and my mates cant get started quickly enough. Mr Rimmer the farmer takes a number of us on his wagon to the field, after telling us he pays two shilling a hamper. We get a hamper, it's huge, it's as big as a shed. After about two hours Bobby and I have managed to fill a corner, some women and their kids have filled a couple. The women have a knack of pulling the whole plant up then run their fingers down it, taking all the pods off in one movement. We try it and seem to make better progress, we also stop eating them, but this just doesn't make any difference, and by the middle of the day we have only managed to almost fill one hamper. "I know, we can put some stones in the bottom, he'll never know," said Bobby. We dragged our hamper over to the wagon to get our tally, we didn't know

Mr Rimmer emptied the hamper, stones and all. "Get back and get me another half-filled hamper boys, or the only thing you'll be getting from me is this pitchfork up you're a---." After working all day we got two hampers filled, two shilling each, a shilling for my Mam and a shilling for me. We only went pea picking a few times after that, the last time we went five of us got a lift back home, it was a Hartleys van that stopped for us, it was open at the back and both sides had trays of shelled peas. On shelves from the floor to the ceiling, I was seeing how far the peas bounced along the road, when the van stopped, "Out you get, all of you, walk." I forgot that vans have wing mirrors. No one talked to me as we trudged our way home. We try some spud picking, this is really back breaking, and we don't last very long, another farmer telling us what he'll do with his pitchfork if we don't move a lot quicker. I can see now why farmers always seem to carry pitchforks around.

BOYS WILL BE BOYS

The nights are closing in now and it's going darker earlier. Always looking for something to do, we heard Mrs Grice telling a neighbour her daughter is terrified of feathers. Bobby and I collect loads of feathers and push them through her letter box and wait for the screams. The only screams that were heard that night were mine, as my Mam battered me. Mrs Grice had seen me and told my Mam. Nitcha told us that the girls who live next door to him, one is fourteen and her sister is sixteen, get a bath about seven o'clock each Saturday. The bathroom window is in the yard, no one can use more than four inches of water, that's a rule, it's rationed at bath time. He tells us that the window pane was broken and fixed with plain glass. Ten minutes to seven on Saturday night, about a dozen little figures are silently crouched on top of a shed like cover, it's to protect the mangle from the weather, the cover is in line with the window. At last one of the girls appears. The window is beginning to steam up, now there's a lot of shoving and pushing to get a better look. Then it happened, the roof caved in, arms and legs were entangled in the old mangle. Panic was everywhere, the girls screaming and doors opening, dogs barking and little boys in a state of panic, each one pulling the other back to get in front. What a hiding you'd get off your Mam for this one, I thought, and most of all, what could you say to the priest in confession. I had a bump on my head as big as a goose egg. I told my Mam I fell off the air raid shelter. "You want to fall off again it might knock some sense in to you, I can't."

THE OASIS

Christmas comes around again, and we go carol singing. Our singing is so bad I'm sure people give us money so they don't have to listen to us, and to get rid of us. Gerry, my younger brother, was in trouble. He crept down the stairs and took the apple from my sisters stocking, and replaced it with an onion. Then when she cried, he told her there's no such thing as Father Christmas. We all try to make a few pennies, to go to the pictures or the baths. I go to the baths pretty often and try my best to swim, I'm the only one who can't. Our Jimmy reckons it might be because I nearly drowned in New Brighton, but I'm not scared. I can dive in and splutter and choke to the other side, but I still can't swim.

There is a pond on Wood's farm field, it's called The Oasis. It's in the middle of the field and there's nothing near it, lots of dead trees are in it. Last summer, when the nights were warm, all the lads peeled off their clothes and swam in it. I went in but made sure I held on to the trunk of a tree. This went on for a few nights until one night I heard a whistle blowing, we heard a shout, "Look out lads, it's the Coppers!" Suddenly there was a dozen nude little boys running for cover to the cornfield next door, the police had our clothes. After about an hour we gave ourselves up, we then got a telling off and told of the dangers of skinny dipping in a pond with so many dead trees in it. A police station is along the lane, it's in Croxteth Hall Lane, and there is another in Meadow Lane. We avoid going near them in case we get locked up, my Mam says never to bring trouble to the door.

UNXPLODED TORPEDO

It's May now and the air raids have gone worse, almost every night the sirens go off, with this frightening up then down wailing noise. It makes the hairs on the back of your neck stand up. We use the shelter that often now I think I know every creepy crawly that lives in there. It's been so full of water that some workmen called, they drained the water away then dug a hole in the floor and cemented it, the water now runs into this. We have less room and it's smelly.

On the wireless we get someone called William Joyce, everyone calls him Lord Haw Haw, he's a traitor who says things like, "Germany calling, Germany calling, hello you people from Scotland Road, did you enjoy getting bombed last night, we shall be over tonight to drop a lot more bombs, enjoy yourselves people of Liverpool, while you may." We're back in the shelter again tonight. We can hear the sound of gunfire, as our guns try to shoot the German bombers down. Searchlights sweep the sky, then we hear them getting nearer and nearer on their way to bomb the docks, and anywhere else, but never our school. The bombing has been going on a couple of hours now, we hear loads of explosions. My Mam says, "I hope our Molly is alright." She's my Mam's sister, my Auntie, she lives off Scotland Road in Hankin Street, this is very close to the docks. As my Mam stops talking there's a noise overhead, it goes shoosh, shoosh, shoosh, we all wait for an explosion, but nothing, then the sound of a whistle. "It's Mr Woods, our air raid warden." "Don't panic, don't panic," he's shouting. He seems to be panicking for all of us. He said he's looking for an unexploded landmine, he disappears into the darkness of our garden. Then there's an almighty scream, he thinks he's fallen into a hole with the mine. I'm secretly delighted, he's a horrible man. He has one daughter who is spoilt. He had a Christmas tree in his window, it was decorated with baubles, when he saw me looking at it, he closed the curtains, this was in the daylight one afternoon. Anyway no such luck, he fell into a hole alright, but it was into a trench we lads had dug. We were playing soldiers, we've got tin hats and the butts from reject rifles Paddy O'Hanlon sells on his cart for firewood. We've been playing soldiers all week. When the all clear sounds Mr Woods appears looking very sheepish to tell us all that it's an aerial torpedo, it's been meant for the river but it's two roads away stuck in Mercer's back garden. Someone says the Luftwaffe must have a cross-eyed bomb aimer. Lots of people have to leave their houses until the bomb disposal unit deals with it.

I'm up very early, I go and tell Mr Harper I can't do the milk this morning, then I call for two mates, we want to see the unexploded torpedo. The streets are roped off, policemen are making sure no one gets near. We go to the end of the roped area and sneak across all the back gardens, we reach next door to Mercers. We are lucky with no man in the house, the garden is overgrown, and no one can see us. The bomb squad are already there. After what seems ages they defuse it. When it was over we cheered. "You little bastards," the officer shouted at us, then he and his soldiers were swamped by loads of women kissing them and giving them bottles of beer.

AUNTY MOLLY

I'm going to see my Aunt Molly today, we have a day off from school. I'm getting the tram to Belmont Road then a tram along to Scotland Road, it costs a penny transfer. I get off the tram at the Rotunda, it's a theatre but today it's in ruins, it's been bombed. Auntie Molly lives opposite in Hankin Street, I hurry along to make sure she's okay, she lives in number ten. Good, it's still there. I knock but get no answer. There's a hole in the door, I put my finger through and feel for a piece of string and with it comes the key. Letting myself in, I like this little house, it still as gas lighting. Upstairs in the attic my grandfather, my Mam's Dad, keeps cages of canaries. He lives with my Aunt Molly and Uncle Peter, but he is always at sea or asleep in the corner. Today he is asleep in the corner, he never heard me knocking. I wonder if he slept when the Rotunda got blitzed. My Aunty Molly comes home, the first thing she says is, "Have you had something to eat?, I'm doing some bacon ribs and cabbage I got from Greaty market, how is your mother?" "She's fine Aunty Molly." "The bombing around here has been terrible, a whole street was hit by a land mine, they had all the bodies laid out on doors waiting for the ambulances, those German bastards. I hope our Pat and our Larry are giving them what for." I think to myself, Uncle Pat yes, but Uncle Larry no, he was only taken back last week by the red caps, the army police, for 'overstaying his leave' as my Mam put it. My grandfather wakes up, probably with the smell of the bacon ribs. "Who's this little feller then Molly?" "He's one of our Annie's lads Dad." I'm nearly nine and he doesn't know me, some grandad I think. Still, I have seen him, I have never ever seen my other grandad, my Dad's father. He had a row with my Dad years ago, my Mam said, and never bothered seeing his grand kids. I get fed by my Aunty Molly. She always gives me a sixpence and puts me on a tram with the words. "Go straight home in case there's a raid."

COCOA LEGS

The young women, because they can't get any stockings, now tan their legs with a colouring. This led up to my Mam giving me a hiding. I was in the house, when I heard the words, "Come here you little swine." "What for Mam?" I said. "I'll give you what for." With that she battered me, then dragged me out to the back door. Mrs Murphy and her daughter Peggy are there, "Wasn't him Mrs Hynes, it's the younger lad," said Peggy. It seems every time she and her friend are going out dollied up, our Gerard follows them shouting, "Ah! Cocoa legs!" My Mam can't take a hiding back so I tell her I'm going to hit him. "You better not my lad or you'll get another one, anyway I'm surprised it wasn't you."

NITTY NORA

We have a note from school. I hate this particular note, the one that tells our Mams that Nitty Nora the head explorer is coming to school. This short note creates panic in our house, right away Mam sends one of us to the chandlers for a bottle of paraffin. This is usually big truck, my elder brother Jimmy, I'm little truck, names my Mam calls us when she means business. These are like 'don't mess with me if you know what's good for you' names.

The paraffin has been bought, the water in the boiler next to the bath has been heated, we wait for the shout, "Right you lot, who's first, come and get your head done. I'm not having any my kids coming home with lousy heads." "Go on, she shouted you," said Gerard. "No she didn't," said Jimmy. "Oh I'll go first," I said, kneeling over the bath. the torture begins. "Keep your head still, don't move," Mam says, then pours the paraffin over my head.It's running down my ears, along my nose, then my Mam scrubs my head like it's the front step. I have to move, it's in my eyes, smack! "Ouch, that hurt that Mam." I get swilled off with a pan of warm water. "Dry your head and wait by the fire, next one!" shouts my Mam. Everyone has had their heads scrubbed now. My Mam sits on her rocking chair, in front of the fire, the Echo newspaper spread across her knees, steel nit comb at the ready. "James, Gerard, Richard, whatever your bloody name is, kneel down here." "Okay Mam, I'm kneeling." Head down, my Mam attacks, the steel comb digging that deep she could have raked a couple of Mr Wood's fields. After a few of her sayings of "I think that's one", and a swift hand movement toward the fire. If you hear a crack it is one, a body as she calls them, maybe the Germans have put little explosives in them.

Next day I visit Nitty Nora. I sit down, she approaches holding a bone at arm's length. She flicks this through my hair, then with a look on her face that says 'I hate little boys and this job', she's finished. "Nice clean boy," she says, in a voice that sounds as if she's disappointed. I should think so I thought, Hitler's storm troopers wouldn't have survived the dreaded paraffin and comb attack. Some kids have notes to take home, they run the gauntlet of lads shouting, "Ah, nitty head!" Mam is well pleased that night when we tell her we are all clean. "Good, it's Saturday tomorrow, she says. "I want you three lads to get your haircut at old Mr Perry's."

THE DREADED BARBER

We are on our way to the barbers, Mr Perry. Jimmy, he's big truck today, is given the money one shilling and sixpence, that's a tanner each. We drag our feet going there, we don't like the barbers, it's at the back of the fish shop and it stinks. On arriving we sit on a bench, waiting our turn. On the window ledge that looks out into the yard are dirty old shaving mugs, blue bottles are struggling on the sticky fly papers and are something to look at until you hear "Next," and Jimmy pushes me forword. "Climb up here, and keep your bloody head still, sending kids in on a Saturday, and some with heads as big as Birkenhead, and all for a bloody tanner." I'm getting told off already and I haven't done anything yet. I climb onto a board he places across the seat, he plonks his big fat belly against the seat and the hair raid begins. He has a woodbine dangling from his mouth, the ash is going to drop off any moment, I turn my head to avoid it. Then he plays a drum roll on my head with the comb and the scissors, muttering, "I said keep bloody still will you." At last he's almost finished. The last thing he always does is set alight a taper then singe what's left of your hair. I wait outside until he's savaged my two brothers' heads.

When they come out we play 'first wet', this is spitting on your hand and clouting each other over the head, this soon gets us home. We're no sooner in the house when we hear the sweet welcoming voice of my Mam, "What the bloody hells that, get back there and tell Sweeney Todd he hasn't took anything off." We are not looking forward to this. "What the hell do you three little sods want?" "Mr Perry, my Mam said you haven't took anything off," said Jimmy. "Haven't took anything off, haven't took anything off, get over here, I'll show your mother how much I can take off for a lousy tanner a head!" With that he started to use the neck shaver on us, but this time right over the top of our heads. It was the first time I wore my balaclava in the summer, my head was cut to ribbons. All my Mam said was, "Oh that's better, it's healthy and it will last."

HALF THE TOWN IS MISSING

Gerry, my younger brother, wants me to take him to see our Mam in work. We are not in school today, it's a holiday. We get the tram into town, the conductor tells everyone to get off the tram when we reach the Adelphi Hotel, the overhead power lines are down from the bombing and there's been lots of buildings hit. We decide to walk to Price Street, that's where Doyles café is. Lewis's store has been hit, also Blackler's store. The police and the firemen won't let anyone pass, so we go a round about way there, hosepipes are everywhere. We cut along Dale Street and into Castle Street, all Lord Street as been hit by the bombs, the smell of burning and smoke is everywhere. We reach our Aunty Lou's café at last and my Mam shouts at me for being so foolish to come into town. We spend some time on the pinball machine, the café is always packed, it's just around the corner from the Sailors' Home. There's seamen from all over the world sailing on the convoys to Russia. The German U-boats wait for them out past Liverpool Bay, lots of men don't come back, their ships being sunk. My Mam sneaks us some chip butties, Aunty Lou won't give you anything, my Aunt Molly says she's as tight as a camel's bum in a sandstorm. We all get a lift home from a delivery driver, he knows all the roads that are still open to traffic.

THREE CHEERS FOR THE NAVY

Back in school a lot of men teachers are excited, listening to the wireless in the staff room. It seems a big German warship, the *Bismarck,* is being hunted in the Atlantic Ocean by ships from the Royal Navy. Mr Thomas keeps popping in and out of class, giving us reports, he is very keen and gets us kids the same way. After a few days it gets trapped and destroyed by lots of our ships. Mr Thomas says this is a big blow to Germany, it was Hitler's pride and joy, and calls for three cheers for the Royal Navy.

THE SNITCH

Mr Thomas told the class to write a composition, oh, I have been told to call it an essay. He said it is to be called The Robin. An older boy I know taught me a silly little poem, I thought I would give my class mates a laugh, so I wrote it in the centre page of my exercise book, the intention being to take the pages out before the teacher collected the books in. I wrote 'The Robin: The robin lives in a rhubarb tree, and whistles like a cow." The lads passed it around, I told them not to pass it to Tucker the snitch, too late. "Sir, Sir, look what Hynes 'as wrote in his book." I am going to kill Tucker when my hand stops stinging. Why do teachers say, "This is going to hurt me more than it's going to hurt you," then whack you? Baker is still in our class, the lad who liked to sit on the mat. When we were in the infants, Mr Thomas asked the other day if anyone in the class had any unusual things to tell. Baker's hand shot up. "Sir, Sir, I have, a bird fell down our chimney, Sir, and it was all dirty with the soot," said Baker. "Did yer catch it?" asked Mr Thomas. "Er! We haven't got a cat Sir, but me and my Mam did Sir, we were really scared." "Sit down lad," was all Mr Thomas said, while the rest of the class tittered.

SOUR GRAPES

My mates and myself don't remember much about grapes, there's none in the shops, but a few days ago we were walking along the top of the wall at the back of West Derby village hall. On one side is woodland and the other side leads to the back of

house. Some have lean-to greenhouses built against the wall and there they were, big bunches of mouth watering grapes, we just had to taste these. After a short time we found out if two lads held another lad's ankles, he could lie flat on the greenhouse roofs and reach the grapes through the air vents. This worked a treat for a time, that is until we decided to let Nitcha go with us. Along the wall we went, but as soon as we reached the greenhouses, with a shout of "there's a bunch", Nitcha ran on to the greenhouse roof, and with a terrible sound of breaking glass he disappeared. Then all hell broke loose. Whistles were blowing as the scout group who where based in the village hall gave chase, they were out to catch the grape robbers. They had no chance, we knew every inch of the woods, also they were posh kids, no chance against us from the corporation houses. Through the woods and over the wall into Meadow Lane, safety was our aim. "Poor Nitcha, he must be cut to pieces," someone said. "Who's telling his Mam?" said another. "We'll all have to tell her," I said. We reached the wall and safety in Meadow Lane. Sitting on a gate with a big bunch of grapes, and an even bigger grin on his face, is Nitcha, not a mark on him. "Hiya lads, anyone want a grape?" Then we jumped on him and ragged him for being so stupid, but mainly for spoiling our grape supply.

THE PIG MUST GO

At Harper's farm, my brother Jimmy and I have heard that a butcher is coming on Thursday to kill one of the pigs. Bill Harper tells me it's to be kept quiet, as they are allowed to kill just one a year for their own use and they have already done this, so this one is to be kept secret, sort of on the black market. As we are in the middle of a school holiday Jimmy and I want to watch. Thursday arrives and my brother and I are at the farm early, he goes on the milk round with Bill, and I help Daddy Harper, this way we can come back and wait for the butcher. He arrives at long last, he's a fat little man, not unlike a pig himself I told Jimmy. He told me to shut up in case anyone heard me and we were chucked out. There's quite a few men around, Jimmy and myself look in from the next sty. The little fat man opens a case and then begins to put the gun together, much like a gangster who is a hit man. By now the pig is squealing because it's being

held down and sat upon by four burly men. The butcher put the gun to the pig's head and pulled the trigger, it never fired. I thought, I hope our soldiers have better guns than that. The fat man fiddled around with the gun, aimed it a few times at a block of wood, he said it was jammed. "I need this done today," Bill said. "I have someone coming a long way for it." After a lot of talking, all the men held the pig down again and the fat man cut it's throat. I and my brother felt sick, the poor pig bled buckets of blood. All Daddy Harper said was, "Good, we'll make some black puddings with that."

THE HOLIDAY

Last week my Mam took us for a week's holiday, paid for by the soldiers and sailors. Mam said it's to help people to have a break.

We went to West Kirby, it's the seaside and it's over the water in the Wirral. We stayed in a nice house, it belongs to a nice lady, she's a Miss. We went to the beach with my Mam, while we there some lads told us that a shark was washed up on the beach at a place called Hoylake. Jimmy and I ran along the beach until we reached the shark, what a disappointment we had, it was only small, and every kid in Hoylake must have carved their initials on the poor thing. When we got back my Mam had gone, she must have thought we knew our way back to the house that we were staying in, but we didn't know and we were on the sands with no shoes or socks on. We decided to find the house. All the roads in West Kirby start looking alike when your lost, but after what seemed ages we found it.

The next day we were invited for our dinner to the biggest house I have ever been in, it belongs to the ex-Lord Mayor. My Mam had pre-warned us about having good manners and to always say please and thank you. After we had eaten our lovely meal, the lady of the house asked me, "Would you like some more?" Being polite and remembering my manners, I replied, "No thank you, I'm full up." "You're what?" said the lady. "I'm full up," I replied. "How cute," she said amidst loads of laughter. Why are they laughing I thought, don't they know good manners? We came home after a week, I was glad, and I think my Mam was, I heard her say, "I couldn't put up with them much longer with their airs and graces."

MY FIRST CHICKEN RUSTLING

I've decided to keep chickens, but I can't buy them, so tonight I shall nick two chickens from a hen hut in a garden next but one to ours. I lie awake until everyone is asleep, then I let myself out of the back door. It's moonlight, no sign of an air raid just a few searchlight sweeping the sky, it's ideal for my commando raid. Crossing next door's garden and scaring their cat, but not half as much as it scares me, I climb over a fence and I'm near the chicken hut, it's not locked. Opening the door very quietly, peering inside, I can just about see the chickens on their perch gently clucking away, half asleep. Quick as a flash, quicker than Brer Fox could, I snatch them and into my sack they go. Making my way back to our yard, now where do I put them? I haven't got any where. At the bottom of our yard is an old dolly tub, Mam doesn't use it because it leaks. Upside down it goes, and the chickens are under. Come tomorrow, I thought, I'll get some wooden boxes from the back of the shops and make a little chicken house. I sneak back into the house, I haven't been missed, everyone is asleep. No sooner than I am up next morning, Peter the boy from next door but one calls. "Do you know what Rick, someone has nicked our two hens."As he is speaking I can hear them fluttering around under the dolly tub. "My Mam is telling the police, we'll know them they are speckled, there's none like them around here." I'm sure the dolly tub is moving as I steer him out of the yard. That night two chickens returned home.

MAM'S COAT

I am still keen on having chickens, but I'll rear them myself. The rag and bone man comes down our street, he has goldfish, and also day old chicks. I love these little balls of fluff, he has them packed in a brown cardboard box. "Hey mister, what do you take for some chicks?" "Any old rags, any old rags," he shouts. That's the same answer he gives us when we shout, "What do you feed your horse on?" "I haven't got any mister," says I. "My Mam makes rag mats with ours, will you take a coat?" "I'll have to see it first son, now run along I'm going soon," he says. I'm back within minutes with the coat and I'm ready to pick which chicks I want, then suddenly slam, bang, I'm knocked all over the street, it's my Mam. "You little bastard, that's my one and only good coat, get in the house now." Despite this set back I do a deal with the Raggy and for a load of jam jars acquired from here there and everywhere, I get my lovely chickens. I do my best to keep them warm, filling a couple of jam jars with warm water. This didn't work very well, next morning two are dead, drowned in the water I put in to keep them warm. Determined not to give up I go to see a mate of mine, Sid, he lives two doors away. His Dad has a small chicken farm, which is on the corner of Oak Lane and Muirhead Avenue. Sometimes they keep day old chicks at home. Under the boiler by their bath he hangs a garden riddle, in it is a mop head. His Dad has hatched eggs from the shops under this, he reckons the chickens cuddle into it, they think it is their Mam and it's warm. His Dad isn't using it so he lends it to me, it works a treat. In no time at all the chickens grow and I move them outside. I don't have a chicken run, but have a little hut that I made myself out of boxes and bits of wood from my favourite suppliers the back of the shops. The chickens roam over everyone's gardens, as quick as the neighbours grow for victory the chickens are eating for victory. Everybody's greens are being attacked. In no time at all, the once little balls of fluff are huge cockerels, taking on all comers, including next door's cat. Even the bin men are wary of them. So many people have complained about them, my Mam says they will have to go.

THE CHICKEN KILLER

I'm at the farm one day and I tell Daddy Harper about them. "Listen son, you're a man now." "I'm only nine Mr Harper," I said. "What I mean son, is that there's a war on you know, and you have to take the place of a man. Come with me." Into the barn we went, as quick as a flash he snatched up a squawking cockerel. Despite it struggling he held it between his knees. "Now my lad, we are having chicken tonight, watch and learn." With that, he twisted its neck. "Now you can help me pluck it while its still warm. There's your answer, go home and help the food rationing out." Now after becoming a chicken rustler. I'm about to become a chicken killer.

At the weekend I'm determined to give my Mam and our family a good meal. I go stalking my now wild cockerels. I'm pretty sure they know something is up, every time I get near one off it gets, over the fences and away for the day. I wait until it's going dark and they go to roost. This works a treat. I now have my first victim, or shall I say family Sunday dinner. Then I have to close my eyes and think it has to be done, there's a war on. I begin to feel I'm evil and in the Hitler Youth movement. It was easier than I thought it would be, I have plucked it and presented to my Mam. She thinks it's wonderful. I asked her to swear she wouldn't tell my brothers or sister where it came from. They all tucked in to it in good style, I couldn't, because of a terrible feeling of guilt. After all, me and the mop head took the place of it's mother between us, from when it was a chick. Nevermind, as Daddy Harper says, these things have to be done, there's a war on you know.

My fame as a chicken killer begins to spread, this is with my Mam talking up the lane, or, as my Dad would say, jangling. "I told Mrs Brown you will kill their chicken, there's no man in the house and they all look like they need a good feed," Mam said. "Hey Mam, I don't want to do any more, anyway Mam their chicken is a pet, it's even got a name, the kids call it Eggo, after the one in the Beano comic. Anyway, Mrs Harper told me that dressing and preparing a bird for the table, sounds better." "I don't care if you dress the chicken, or undress the chicken, just go round there and do it, there's a few coppers for you she said." Over the next few weeks everybody seems to be eating a lot better, and the chicken population gets smaller. Our chickens are down to one, a little black plump chicken. It has a small comb, I'm convinced it's a hen. Nitcha and I go down Croccy, we know where the gamekeeper keeps some dummy eggs, then we make a nesting box, from an orange box. These are great for making things. I put straw in it and the dummy egg to encourage the hen to lay, every morning for weeks I'm up early waiting for it's first egg, then one morning, it stretched up and crowed, just a little cock a doodle do, but that was enough to seal it's fate. "Mam, you know that hen in our back?" "Don't tell me it's laid an egg at last son." "No Mam, that hen is a cockerel, its just crowed, we'll have it at the weekend Mam." At the weekend my Mam set about plucking it, and I heard her tell Mrs Harrison, "As I plucked it, there was feathers and fleas everywhere. When I finished there wasn't a pick on it, there was more meat on our Richard, it was just a head with a pair of legs on it. I said throw it in the bin, I'll open that tin of corn beef I have put away.

GERMAN SPIES

The war goes on. My Dad is stationed in Scotland now, on the Isle of Skye. The little gang of us are now following telegraph boys to see whose house they will call at with a telegram. It's usually bad news saying someone is missing in action. We also chase after ambulances, one stopped in the next road to ours, a man had hanged himself. I saw him. his head was swollen, he still had a piece of rope around his neck, and his eyes were bulging. I told my Mam. She said I shouldn't be running after ambulances. Don't worry, I wont be after that. We have a new game now, any man who has a beard and carries a little case, well, he's got to be a German spy. We follow them everywhere, one man for a week, until one day he called at Mrs Smith's house. When we asked Reggie Smith who he was, he said "Oh, he's the insurance collector."

RIDING THE TRAMS

Unknown to my Mam, I go with my mates legging leccies, these are the electric tram cars. We sit on the back bumper, we have positions. There is first sitty, then second sitty - you hang on to the lamp, then third, also standy up, this is your fingers go in to the slots under the stairs and your feet on the wooden slats under the tram. When another tram passes the wind almost knocks you off. First and second sitty are the worst. If it's a woman conductor you're okay, but if it's a man, they hit you with the trolley rope, they lean out of the door and can lash out as far as second sitty. We are coming to the end of summer now, this to most people means dark nights and the blackout, but to us kids it's conker season and plenty of raids on orchards. If we go to Gillmoss past Baldwin's farm, on the other side of the lane is a little church, it's called St Swithens. It has two apple trees in the grounds and the apples look very tempting, but it's a Catholic church and we are nearly all Catholic lads. We don't touch the apples for fear of being struck down, so two lads who are Protestants get sent in. Further along the lane as it bends towards the East Lancashire Road there is a slaughter house, we climb up onto a ledge and watch the pigs getting killed. Each lad swears not to eat any more bacon. Then when my Mam fries it, the temptation is too much. Vows are made to be broken, when there's a bacon buttie to be eaten.

THE SPUD MINE

My Mam says she can't get any potatoes, there is a shortage, so she tells us to go and see if there is any place we can buy some. There are about seven of us. Mam tells me to take Gerry my younger brother, she and the other lad's Mams give us some coppers. After walking for a while we manage to hitch a lift on the back of a lorry, it takes us along the East Lancashire Road to Knowsley. A shop in the village is selling five pound of spuds to each customer. Gerry decides to get another five pound, so he borrowed a lad's glasses and another lad's cap, I was expecting him to get chased, but he got away with it. Finding it hard to hitch a lift home, we decide to walk across the fields. Not far from home we came across a long mound of soil shaped like a long pyramid. Scraping away some soil then straw, suddenly it appeared, a spud mine, tons and tons of spuds. We filled our bags and jerseys with as many as we could carry, then swore to each other not to tell anyone else. Struggling home with our load of spuds we gave these to our Mams. "My they're a good five pounds of spuds," my Mam said. "Are you sure their scales are working?" Next day we went knocking on people's doors taking orders for spuds, we get lots of orders, and lots of spuds. We've got money for the pictures and the baths, also the chippy. Alas, all good things come to an end. After a few weeks the farmer is waiting for us with his dogs, plus a shotgun under his arm. The lads spot him before he sees us. It was good while it lasted.

THE YANKS JOIN THE WAR

It's coming up to Christmas again. My Mam received some parcels from the Whittaker family in Canada. I got a frog aeroplane, it looks good. You assemble it yourself and put a drop of gasoline in it, then it flies. After finding out that gasoline is an American way of saying petrol, I pester my Mam for it, but she insists I wait until Christmas, otherwise I'll have nothing on Christmas day. I'm on the milk round as much as I can, I'm hoping to get a few tips for Christmas. I don't have much chance as old Jones's and Daddy Harper pick all the houses that tip, I can't compete for being crafty against a Welshman and a Yorkshire man. My Mam says the same two would pinch the nuts off their monkey. She buys his baccy for him the cheapest you can buy, it's called Beano. You get a free clay pipe when you buy it. She said he would smoke horse shit if he thought it would save him money. Me and the lads go carol singing, we get some money despite lots of people telling us to come back because it's too early. There's only two days to go, it can't be too early, we think they mean no, so we give them a verse of "If you haven't got a penny a halfpenny will do, if you haven't got a halfpenny God bless you." People are saying that the Japanese have bombed an American Naval base called Pearl Harbour and America is at war.

It's Christmas once again, but this time, besides the apple and orange in a sock, there is a wonderful model aeroplane. I start to put it together. I can't wait to fly it. I need a drop of petrol, a mate of mine's brother has a motor bike, and he siphoned a drop for me, now I can't wait to fly it. I'm that keen I can't wait to go to a field, so followed by about twenty kids who are as keen to see it make its maiden flight and soar into the sky I release it in our side garden. The field is too far away, it soared alright unfortunately smack into the side of the house. All the way from Canada to be destroyed in seconds. I ran in to tell my Mam. "You wouldn't be much good as a pilot, would you lad," is all she said.

STEERIES AND WINNY WARMERS

Christmas passes and the war goes on. My Dad comes home on leave, he has a few balaclavas for us. Most kids have these in the winter, some are air force blue, some navy blue, but most are khaki. My Dad's posting has been changed, he's in Lincolnshire with bomber command. He's also left us a nice warm service great coat, which Gerry and I have on our bed. Most people around here have an army greatcoat on the bed, those who say they don't must have a navy or an air force one. After all, there's a war on you know, make do and mend, every one says. Most kids wear hand me downs, these are clothes that their elder brother or sister have grown out of.

We kids play out a lot in the street, making steeries, these are steering carts. The hardest part of making a steery is getting the old pram wheels. One way we have found successful is to go over people's back yards at night. If we see an old pram we knock at the house the next day and ask the woman can we have it to make a trek cart for the boy scouts. Then we find a plank of wood, a wooden box, a big nut and bolt and washer, usually supplied by one of the lad's sisters who works in a factory, and a piece of rope for steering. We borrow a saw from Mr Sumner, he seems to be the only one who has a saw, perhaps not the only one, but he's the only one who will lend us a saw. He is a nice man, he always has time for us lads. Despite having only one arm he has the nicest clipped privets for miles, he has hand clippers with a spring in them, he and his privets are so nice we don't practise our parachute jumping in them at night. Some of us have a jam jar on our steery with a lit candle in it, until the old A.R.P warden catches us, then it's "Put them bloody lights out, do you want us all bombed to smithereens?" Nitcha says to me, "What's a smithereen?" "I don't know," I said. "But I don't want to be one, blow the candles out Nitch." "Hey! Rick, what does A.R.P. stand for?" Nitcha asked. "I don't know Nitch, my Dad said it means Always Ready for a Pint."

We try to keep warm by making winter warmers. We find a fairly large tin, knock some holes in it, tie wire on it for the handle, fill it with wood or nick some coal, set it alight, then swing it overhead until it's glowing. I then wonder if the German bombers might get their bearings from our winny warmers. "Look Fritz, those people with their little fires, we must be over Liverpool." Sometimes you get a dozy lad who walks into another lad's winny warmer, probably because of his balaclava blocking his vision, and scatters burning embers everywhere, then gets duffed up for spoiling it, never giving a thought for his burnt head.

STREET GAMES

We play lots of games, the most favourite with the lads is pie crust. One lad stands against the wall, he's the anchor man, the rest of your team stoop down holding onto the lad in front, then the other side run and jump onto your backs. If you can shake them off before the count of ten it's your turn, if you all collapse they go again. The girls can't play that, it's too rough, so we play alallio with them. When it's their turn to be out and we have to catch them, they're always caught easy. When we're out it's for hours, it becomes a bore so we don't bother letting them play. Games we also play are ones called kick the can or comics, then there's kerb or wall, stroke the bunny, sometimes catch a girl kiss a girl. If the girl's ugly we pretend we can't catch her. Girls are better playing their own games such as skipping or rounders. When it's light nights some of the mothers and big sisters put a big rope across the street, and loads join in, singing "All in together to see Cinderella, when I count twenty the rope must be empty, five, ten, fifteen, twenty," or "On a mountain stands a lady, who she is I do not know." Some of my mates think I'm a sissy because I know a lot of these songs, but I know lots of songs, some with the wrong words, to the tune of Rule Britannia. We sing "Rule two tanners, two tanners make a bob, three make eighteen pence and four two bob," or While Shepherds Watch their

Flocks, we sing "While shepherds wash their socks by night, all seated around the tub, a block of Sunlight soap came down, and they began to scrub". To the tune of Music While You Work we sing "Mussolini bought a shirt, Hitler wore it, Chamberlain saw it, that's why war's declared." Vera Lynn sings, "We'll meet again," lots of kids change the words to "Whale meat again." Mrs Harrison calls and tells my Mam, "Them bloody Japaneses have got our poor Georgie, anderem, you know Annie them little yeller fellers, anderem, he's a prisoner of war now."

THE ROOKERY

The dark nights are passing and the evenings are getting lighter. It's also getting warmer, I'm glad, I'm fed up with always being cold. We never have gloves, just old socks on our hands. Even the house is cold in the winter. It has a tiny fire, if you get too near my Mam or Dad says, "Get back, let the monkey see the rabbit", whatever that means I don't know. We are back to our walks down Croxteth Hall Lane and into Lord Sefton's Estate. Every morning and evening the sky overhead is full of, no not enemy aircraft, crows. They have a rookery in the woods along Meadow Lane. Down the stile as we call it, the stile we climb over, then along a footpath. The noise at this time of the year is usually deafening, not today though, the gamekeeper's had a shoot yesterday and the woods are quiet. We climb over the wall to see the dead crows, someone is already there. As we creep through the bushes, they have lit a fire. Creeping closer we see it's Nitcha and another lad, he has a stick and with it he spears dead crows, feathers and all, thrusting them into the fire. They come out like cooked chickens, these he feeds to a huge greyhound that's been with him for days. Then, being him, he said, "Look Rick, Our Lord on the cross." When I looked he had a huge crow attached by it's wings to a gate, it's head was hanging down. Why he does things like he does I don't know, he can be a nice lad, helping a woman to carry her shopping home and yet think nothing of blowing a frog up with a straw or dropping the owl's eggs off the bridge. Then I think he hasn't screwed a chickens neck so I can't call him.

THE HARE

The big greyhound seems to have adopted us. Whatever time we go on our little afternoons out it appears. We don't mind, it's a lot of fun. We go along the lane that starts in Croxteth Hall Lane and comes out in West Derby Village. On each side are private fields and woods. There is a man driving a tractor, he's almost ploughed the field. Over to his left one of the lads spots a hare, pointing it out to the greyhound. Not thinking for a second the dog would see it, let alone chase it, with a mighty bound the dog took off. The hare had a few hundred yards start, over the ploughed field they went, the hare reached the safety of the woods, so it thought, we could still see the dog dodging around the trees, then out of the trees it came, dragging this huge hare along. The man in the tractor was chasing after it, and the dog was chasing after us. We legged it into West Derby Village with the greyhound still carrying the hare, and the man in the tractor still chasing after us. He gave up at Muirhead Avenue, we left the dog with the hare and never saw it again.

NITCHA DIGS FOR VICTORY

We saw our first Yanks yesterday, leaning on a ledge outside of a little shop in the village. "Any gum chum?" That was the first thing that Nitcha asked, they didn't even answer him. "Maybe they don't understand our accent," said one of the lads. "More likely they don't understand Nitcha," I said. "They're not as good as our soldiers, we got loads of things from ours," said another. "They're stationed in the camp our soldiers left in Croccy, we'll go tomorrow," I said.

Next day we tell our Mams we've been to Mass, seeing it's a Sunday. "Funny how you're last out the house and always the first back when it's Mass, let me catch you telling lies, and I'll stiffen you my lad," said my Mam. Some funny sayings my Mam has. We get to the camp, we haven't been here for ages. It's not like when our soldiers had it, then it was smart and tidy, even the stones around the paths were white washed. Now it's untidy, no one comes out of the cook house. Looking in a bin we find a couple of books with nude women in them. The books are called The Naturist, we have a good look at them then hide them for next time we come back. Leaving the army camp we carry on past the gamekeeper we call Plus Four's house, the one who keeps the hounds. Opposite the house and across the lane he has a big wooden shed, it's where he keeps lots of stuff for hunting and tools for use on the estate. Last year Nitcha and myself thought that we saw some birds eggs in a cabinet as we peeped through the gaps in the boards. "I'm having them la," he said. "Give us a legger up to that window." Through the little gap he went, then he dropped down on to the floor. Lucky for him the floor wasn't concrete as he seemed to drop a long way. Over to the cabinet he went, then through a gap in the wall he whispers, "They're only dummies." Then he realised he can't get out, it's built up on the side he got in and he's got no chance of getting out, try as he does it's impossible. "Rick don't leave me will you?" I'm on watch outside we have been here for ages, it's going dark now and I'm scared. Opposite there is a tree, it has lots of skeletons hanging from it, when Plus Fours shoots magpies or crows or kills stoats or anything he thinks might harm the pheasants. He hangs them from the tree, as if to say,mess with me and you hang on the tree. Over time the bones are bleached, at the moment the moonlight is shining through the trees onto them and I'm scared. "Rick, you won't leave me will you?" "No Nitch." I'm thinking about the hiding my Mam will give me when I go home. "Nitch," I whisper. "The floor is soil and there is a shovel in there, go to the front and dig a tunnel, be as quiet as you can." After what seemed ages Nitches head appeared, we ran all the way home. All the street had been out looking for us. My Mam didn't give me a go along, as we call it, all she said was get a wash and get up the dances.

We go for a walk today, and pass the gamekeeper's hut where Nitcha was locked in. There's a small brick building, about fifty yards away. Today three men are sitting outside, they have strange clothes on, bright clothes with different coloured squares and triangles sewn on. They're very friendly, much friendlier than the Yanks. They show us photos of some kids and keep saying bambinos. We realise then they are Italian prisoners and they work on the farm. The clothes are really weird, if they run away they will stick out a mile. We find out that they're locked up at night in the brick building. We visit them a lot during the summer, they always insist in sharing a loaf of bread with us. They are nice men and our little gang like them.

MESSING ABOUT

As the year moves into spring then summer, I still look for ways to make the odd coppers that we need for the pictures or the baths. We now find along Oak Lane and in the fields that parts of the tall grass along the sides of the lane are flattened. This usually means that the yanks have been courting their lady friends. We often find money and cigarettes that spill from their pockets. One day a pair of drawers was hanging from a bush, and for a laugh Nitcha said, "Hey Tommo, they're your sisters, I saw them on your washing line, one yank and there off." Tommo jumped on Nitcha who made it worse by shouting, "No they're not, I forgot she doesn't wear any."

Now and again we go to the Pier Head and cross the river on the ferry. We then walk along to New Brighton and mess around on the sand. Other days we have a bottle of water and some jam butties, then get the bus to Thurstaston. We play on the hills, and on the common. A few weeks back we found a wasps nest in the ferns. Someone had the idea of smoking them out. Tying some dry grass on a stick, we set it alight and shoved it down the hole where the wasps had a nest. It seemed to be working, until after a few minutes the whole of the common seemed to burst into flames. We tried to stamp it out, even smacking the flames with our coats, but it got worse. We ran off when we heard the fire engine, also because we were being attacked by a swarm of angry wasps. We only wanted to smoke out the wasps, unfortunately we almost smoked out the people of Thurstaston.

THE KITE MAKERS

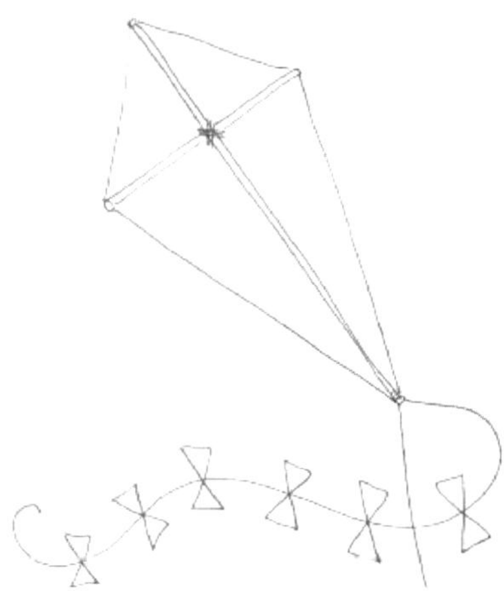

I'm now making kites. I get three small garden canes, some grease proof paper, and string. The canes are tied together to make a frame. Around the outside edge string is tied, then the paper is cut out to the shape of the frame. Making a paste with flour and water, we stick it around the frame. A tail is made with string and twirls of paper, and on the end is tied a rag for ballast. These fly so well that loads of kids want them. I start making them with Jimmy Boyle, after all he showed me how to make them, plus his sister gets us the greaseproof paper and string from where she works. We sell them for half a crown each, Jimmy and I are in the money again, the kites are great flyers. They soar high into the sky, and the money into our pockets. Then our little business fizzles out. Our little gang like to make things, catapults are popular, or catties as we call them. We look for a forked branch on a tree, it's got to be even, then look around for elastic, mostly cut from an old tyre inner tube. Sid and I go taking shots at the rats on his Dad's chicken farm.

CHICKEN RUSTLING STINKS

I want to keep chickens again, but this time I want laying hens. I manage to get some wire netting from Harper's Farm, I don't think they want it, but just to make sure I wait until it's dark. I get one of my mates to help me, and with the help of Mr Sumner's tools make a little chicken hut with a run, and a little ladder for them to run up when they want to lay. We feel good after making this, but we haven't got any hens, so along we go to Oak Lane to Wright's pig farm. We often see hens in the lane, there's a gap under the gate and they come out into the lane. Today we're going to encourage them to come further out in the lane, and to help us we have bread in our pockets for bait. Even though it's summer we wear a jersey each. Bobby and I take up our positions by the bushes in the lane, the bread we have trailed from the gate to past the bushes. We wait, and soon there's some movement under the gate. The bread has been spotted and along the lane they come. "What colour do you want?" whispers Bobby. "Any colour, I whisper back. "Even a striped one if you see one." Nearer and nearer they come, with a peck here and a peck there, now they're running trying to beat each other to the next piece of bread. Suddenly Bobby shouts "Now!" The two of us grabbed at the same time, the noise is deafening, under our jerseys go the hens. Someone must have heard that row, but no one came, it's a pig farm so they must be used to hearing lots of noise. Into their new home they went. Mam asked me where did I get them, I told her we found them in a field miles from anywhere. "You probably found them before they were lost knowing you, woe betide you if someone comes knocking at this door for them." After weeks no eggs arrive. Sid, who's Dad has the chicken farm, says they're too young to lay, they're pullets. I can't wait forever, so I have decided to go chicken rustling again.

Next to Harper's farm in Hornspit Lane there is a cottage, in it lives a little stooped man who to me looks like a Goblin. He keeps chickens, one of which gets under the fence and mixes with the farm chickens. I'm fascinated with this hen, it is unusual to look at being that it's completely black. I read about it, it's a black Minorca. With my mate Alwyn Roberts, who I often take to the farm with me, we decide to catch it. Every day it comes feeding into the barn. We get a big sieve which is used to sort out the potatoes from the chats the small ones, also a pole and a rope. We manage to get some corn, then set a trap in the barn. The sieve is set up with the pole and to this we tie the rope. We are hidden away, we wait and wait, chickens come, eat the corn we replace it. We stay for ages, we are just about to give up when around the corner and into the barn, pecking here and there, comes the Black Minorca. Nearer and nearer it comes, a quick tug on the rope the sieve comes down and she's ours. We tie her legs together and toss her into an old shed in the orchard. Sneaking back undercover of darkness and into the shed, the hen is still fluttering around until we put it into a sack. On the way home there is a terrible smell from the sack. Alwyn reckons the sack as had fertiliser in it. We reach home and untie the hens legs. Into the run it goes, the sack goes into the bin, the sooner the better we thought.

Next morning I go to see how the Black Minorca is and the smell is still on it, then I realise some dirty kid has done one in the old shed the Black Minorca was fluttering around in all day. To cap it all, my Mam grabbed hold of me after a few days. "Get that bloody chicken back up to Mrs Harper, you always make a show of me lad." It seems my Mam called in Harper's to pay her milk bill, and Mrs Harper asked, "How are Ricky's chickens?" "Fine," says my Mam. "Does he have any new ones?" "Oh yes he has," Mam replied. "Is it black?" Mrs Harper asks. "Yes it is," says my mother. "Does it have a black beak, black feet, in fact is black all over?" "Yes Mrs Harper, it does." "Well tell him to get it back here, it's mine." That night the Black Minorca, smell and all, went over Harpers wall. It wasn't hers really but I could not tell her that because it certainly wasn't mine. It might be I should have told her it followed me home, like in the song. "Don't put my boy in prison never any more to roam, he didn't steal your chicken, the bloody thing followed him home."

THE RABBIT BREEDER

There is no sign of the pullets laying so I have swopped them for a rabbit. The lad I swopped with reckons that it will have baby rabbits, so off I go to Lark Hill Library. It's in the mansion house, which is the same building I go to for the Boy Scout meetings. I borrowed a book on rabbits, I read that baby rabbits are called kittens, I thought this was just cats. When they are about to have their babies they start munching straw or hay, then make a nest. The night they are having the kittens lots of soft fur from under her belly is scratched off, with this she lines the nest. This rabbit is Dutch, it is black and white. I made a hutch from an orange box. It already has two compartments. I just put a hole in the centre piece a door on one side and wire netting on the other, just in time because she is already munching the straw, taking it through the hole. I can't resist looking in, she is making a nest, but next time I look she as mucked it up. The book reckons you should not disturb them, so I leave her in peace. After a few days I notice lots of bits of fur so very carefully I open the door, there is a nest and amid the fur are little baby rabbits, they have no fur and look like little baldy mice. I'm so delighted I tell all my mates, they call and every one has a peep. I climb over the allotments and give the mother rabbit some nice fresh carrots.

Next day I peep in to the hutch and the nest is destroyed, half eaten baby rabbits are thrown everywhere, I feel sick. The book did say do not disturb. I'm determined not to give in breeding rabbits, so I decide to help myself. During our little travels in the country side we see a little market garden, the man who it belongs to keeps lots of rabbits, row after row of tea chests with wire front doors. Nitcha and I decide to nick a rabbit. Under the cover of darkness we sneak into the garden, it's moonlight tonight so we can see what we're doing. Moving along the tea chests I spot the one I like. "Do you think that looks like a buck Nitch?" I whispered. "Err! What's a buck la?" "A male," I answered. "How can you tell"? He asked. "It usually has a muzzy and wears kecks." Then I grabbed the rabbit, it squealed. I'd never heard a rabbit squeal, it must have thought I was a stoat. Then we ran. I'm running along the lane with the rabbit stuck down my jersey, suddenly there's a man on a bike along side me. "Okay son give it back," was all he said. No cuff around the ear hole, nothing, then he asked me why I stole it. I told him I keep rabbits, then he asked me why didn't I knock and ask him. "Because you would have chased me." "Ask me now," he replied. "Please mister, can I keep the rabbit?" "Oh go on you little scallywag, but don't steal in future." With that he rode off up the lane.

THE FLEMISH GIANT

On the milk round there lives an elderly gentleman, Mr Roberts. He asks me if I would like a rabbit, it belonged to his son who is now on active service, and does not want it anymore. I'm delighted, Mr Roberts took me into his back garden and there it is the biggest rabbit I've ever seen. "It's a Flemish Giant, and it's a buck," Mr Roberts said. "You can have the hutch as well," he said. I went right away to borrow a cart off Sid, he came to give me a hand. His little cart always stinks, he collects horse muck for his Dad's rhubarb. No horse can escape Sid's ears, he can hear a horse plop from streets away. In no time at all we had the hutch and the rabbit home in our back garden. "Why don't you put the Dutch rabbit in with it, see if they will make babies," said Sid. "Do you mean mate them?" I said. I learnt that from my book. "They might not want to be mates, just good friends," said Sid. "Oh throw it in," I said. This we did, and in no time at all, the hutch was shaking like an old tramcar going down Low Hill.

After a few weeks my black and white rabbit started making a nest again. We left her well alone, and this time she had seven little rabbits. Now I thought I'm in business. I sold most of these when they were big enough, then I spread the word that my Flemish Giant buck was ready to mate with any lad's doe, at a fee. This was either a small payment or a comic, mostly it was a comic, but it had to be a Yanky comic, these were highly prized. My collection of comics soon grew, Captain Marvel, Superman, Batman. I never realised there was so many lads keeping rabbits in the neighbourhood. My buck rabbit never let me down, he was like Super Rabbit doing his bit for the war effort. More rabbits, more rabbit pie.

COLLEGE PUDDING

I felt pretty nervous one day last week. I sat for the scholarship. It was in the Collegiate College, which is in Shaw Street, I didn't know anybody at all. I will know if I pass in a few weeks time. My Mam told me to put a Catholic school for first choice if I pass. Lots of lads have said, what do you want to be a college pudding for? I don't really but if I am, I am. I still go about with the lads. Bobby calls for me and asks do I want to see something funny, but I have to promise I won't laugh until we are outside of the house. He has a sister, Sally, she's eighteen. He is running an errand to tell her friend what time she'll meet her for the dance. We arrive at the house and the mother calls us in. "Go through to the front Bobby," says Mrs Owen. Bobby drags me with him. I knew Millie had no hair because Bobby had told me. Millie had a turban on her head, and on the chair, smoking his pipe and reading the Echo, sat Mr Owen wearing Millie's wig, while Millie stood styling it. It was funny because Mr Owen is bald, to see him reading the Echo so calmly with a head of hair was funny, but I felt sorry for Millie. What if she was doing the jitterbug and the wig fell off?

My Mam is in a good mood, the gasman came today, this meant she got a rebate. We like watching the man when he empties the meter. He turns the cash box upside down on the table, then he counts the pennies. Then quick as a flash he flicks them with his finger into his hand. When he has twelve, which is a shilling, he wraps them in blue paper. When he's finished counting, he takes what he wants, then gives my Mam so many back, but in my Mam's share are quite a few foreign coins. These go back in the meter before the man has even left the street.

STICKLE BACKS AND JAM JARS

We all go fishing a lot. If we go to Newsham Park, we often fish in the smallest lake for Jack Sharps, these are small fish. By pulling a pearl button along in the water with a piece of cotton they swim along chasing it, then we net them. Also we tie a piece of cotton on a stick use a matchstick for a float, tie on a worm, then wait until the fish takes the worm well down it's throat, then yank it out. Jam jars and milk bottles are used to carry them home, most are dead before we reach home, then the rest die the next day.

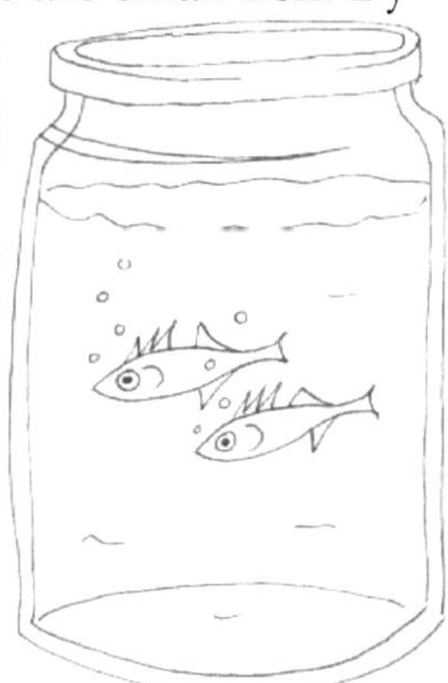

Our best fishing is on Lord Sefton's estate, but it's private. We fished there one time in a pond at the edge of the wood. The fish were queuing up to be caught.Then came the shout, "Look out! Here's a Gamie!" Then it was everyone for himself. Panicking, I jumped over a barbed wire fence, but not high enough, and gashed my knee. Running across the field to the safety of the lane, I looked back. My younger brother Gerard was caught by his jersey on the barbed wire. Oh no! I thought, my Mam will kill me, I'm supposed to be looking after him. The gamekeeper approached him and to every lad's surprise unhooked him and let him go. Usually you expected a good hiding. On reaching the lane Gerard said, "He let me go, because I had my cubs jersey on."

Now that we are safe, Gerard from the gamekeeper and me from the trouble I would have been in if anything should happen to our Gerard, I notice how deep the cut is on my knee. After cleaning the blood off in a stream, one of the gang tied a rag around the gash. We took ages going home. When my Mam saw my knee, she took me to see the A.R.P. warden. I expected him to put salt in it. "This should have had stitches in it, but it's too late now," he snarled, but he did put a clean bandage on it. Then I tried it on with my Mam, I suddenly found it was hard to walk. "Mam, can I stay off school tomorrow, I cant walk properly." "Can you hop?" "Err! Yes Mam." "Well you hop there lad, and back as well." My Mam has a letter to say that I had passed the scholarship, and I am now a college pudding. At the start of the new term I am to attend Saint Elizabeth's Central School for Boys, situated in Breckfield Road South. My Mam says, "I'll have to see if I can get a grant for your uniform, and you'll need new shoes." "Mam, you can save on the cap, I wont be wearing it," I said. "You will, even if I have to glue it on your head." "Alright Mam, see if you can get me one that fits in my pocket."

WHEN MAM WAS A GIRL

Some nights when the wireless isn't working, either because the accumulator hasn't been taken to be charged or we are waiting for my Dad's next leave so he can try to fix it, he always does, usually by sticking the poker in the fire and using it as a soldering iron, or maybe Mam hasn't anything to read, then she tells me about when she was a little girl. Her family lived next door to my Dad's family in Vauxhall Road, this is down by the docks. Her Dad, like lots of men living around there, went to sea. In his early days she said he was on sailing ships, with all the rigging, in fact he was a rigger, which meant a lot of climbing. When steam came in he was a donkey man. I wondered why they had donkeys on board a ship, but she told me the engine was called a donkey engine and he looked after it. After many trips to New York, he would bring her home a pair of patent leather shoes, these were very fashionable and she was the envy of all the little girls in the streets around. She tells me that many men fought with each other, usually through having too much drink. She was always first out to watch these fights, most of them being settled on a Sunday morning in the Loch fields alongside the canal, the same canal my Dad told me the boys would swim in and play ciggies, this meant swimming on your back, so you can imagine what the ciggies were.

Mam told me that she had two uncles who lived with them, they were brothers John Doyle and Peter Doyle. They would bounce her on their knees when she was little. They were she said fine young men, both were lost at sea when the *Lusitania* was sunk by a German submarine just off the coast of Ireland. On her way home to Liverpool from America she was nicknamed the Lucie by a lot of the crew who came from Liverpool. When the news came that she had been sunk, mobs wrecked the local German pork shops. Mam says she felt so sorry for these people they were kind and often gave away soup and ribs to the poor.

Another night my Mam told me about her cousin who lived in Ireland in the city of Dublin. She was shot dead as she looked out of her window, she was shot by the Black and Tans. Mam said they were all rogues let out of prison and put into British army uniforms. Murdering bastards, they were hated by everyone, she said. She also tells me about when the police were on strike, people began eating a lot better, a lot of shops and warehouses were being looted, then the army was brought in to guard these places. Bits of kids was all they were on guard with fixed bayonets, Mam said, and lots of women feeling sorry for them were giving them mugs of tea, probably with lots of sugar, seeing that Tate and Lyles the sugar mill was only over the road. Later when the strike was over, the police began house to house searches looking for stolen goods. Mam said that the entries between the houses were full of stuff people tossed over their yard walls to get rid of. Months later when everything had calmed down, some of the well known families, who didn't have two pennies to rub together, began opening little shops around the neighbourhood.

Mam says we should be glad we live in Norris Green where people are not overcrowded, because when she was little they had the night men, these were men who would walk into wherever you lived, and check how many people were sleeping in the place. If there were too many then you would be fined or even go to jail. She says everyone in the streets looked out for each other. If the night men were spotted a cry would echo through the streets, it was "Cover yourselves up girls, here come the night men!" Then there would be a lot of scrambling over walls as people went to hide away until they got the all clear.

SAINT LIZZIES

My first week at my new school Saint Elizabeth Central School for Boys is a big disappointment, in fact it's horrible, compared to Monksdown Road Council School. It's only the first day but it feels like I have gone back in time to the days of Charles Dickens. As only a small piece of the school yard is flagged, the rest is a mixture of ash and muck. This seems to have encouraged a game called Italiano, a game that involves making a sort of muck pie. Having a knife or some sharp tool, the idea then is to flick the knife or sharp tool into the muck pie from each finger, then your wrist, elbow, shoulder, chin, nose. You finish up aiming the knife through your fingers, your hand being spread out. These games go on all over the school muck yard. My elder brother is a pupil here, a lad in his class has only the one arm. I ask my brother is this the result of him being a poor Italiano player.

We are taught by De La Salle brothers, I'm told this means brothers of the class. Brother Oswald, he's the headmaster, Brother Ambrose the English teacher, Brother Alpheus teaches French, and Brother Edwin history. What about this one for a mouthful - Brother Anastatius, art. There are other teachers I don't know their names yet, but I have a feeling they'll know mine first. The weeks pass by, I ask my brother why he didn't tell me how horrible the school is. He likes it, he said, and he's won a place in Saint Edwards College which is the cream he reckons. I won a place here, I hate to think what I would have got if I had lost. I sat for the eleven plus in the Collegiate college because I went to a council school, for choice I put down St Elizabeth's because it's a Catholic school, also my brother is here.

The school dinners aren't nice, you eat them mainly because it's them or nothing. The rice pudding is made with watered down milk, the enamel bowls it's served in are chipped, they have a blue black colour showing through. This doesn't bother me, but I keep wondering if over time the white enamel that should be on the bowls has been eaten in the rice by some past unsuspecting pupils. Oliver Twist and his mates had better bowls with their food in than these. We were going over the road to Maggie's chippy, but the powers that be found out and now lock the doors. Any boy found eating chips or even smelling of chips receives lines, or the strap.

The school is in Breckfield Road South, around the corner from Breck Road, at the rear of the Royal Cinema. I did hear that the reason a boy's school has a girl's name is that it was once a place for naughty girls, until they moved to new premises in Freshfield. De La Salle brothers took it over to teach the sons of the working class of Liverpool, that was about eighteen years ago. As part of our school uniform I'm supposed to wear a cap, this is stuck almost permanently in my pocket. Me and my mates believe only posh kids wear caps, and they're all cissies. We've always snatched their caps and tossed them over the nearest wall. We wear a blazer and on the badge are the Latin words Semper Fidelis, I'm told this is the school motto, which translates in English to Always Faithful, I always thought that it was dogs that are faithful. Some lads have new leather satchels, but most of us have an army gasmask bag to put our work in.

I get the tram to school, and jump off at Boundary Lane near Ogdens, which is the tobacco works, it really stinks. I walk along Boundary Lane or one of the Rock Streets. There's Grey, Red, or White Rock Street, at the top of these streets is a sweet factory, Barker and Dobson's, and this time the smell is nice. Sweets are on ration now so we make do with the smell. There are very few sweets about now, kids make do with cocoa and sugar, or chew sticky lice. It's not lice as in your head, it's a root of a tree, and it tastes sweet. I don't go on the milk round on schooldays now, just weekends. My brothers and I share bringing the milk can home. I still go to the farm a lot, especially if it's raining or cold. I call these Harper's days, days when I can be in the cow shed nice and warm or play in the loft. I was in the cow shed when one of the cows suddenly started making a lot of noise, she was standing up and a calf was being born, it was hanging from her. I panicked, ran straight in to the house Bill and his Dad Mr Harper followed me. They looked after the cow and her baby, then I realised where the calf would end up in a few weeks and felt sick.

I go to school now with a lad called John Kelly, he hates the school as well, but he's getting bullied by a lad in a senior class. John is a big lad, I can't see why he puts up with this, but because the lad is older than John and in a senior class, he thinks he should be scared of him. Each afternoon we finish school the lad waits for John, today is no different. "Get over here Kelly now, while I duff you up," shouts the bully. Most mornings coming to school with John I have been telling him to lose his temper and jump on the bully, pretend he's called your mother names John, you'll kill him, he wont come near you again. At last it's worked, with a roar like a wounded animal John jumped on the bully. He battered him so much that lads had to pull him away, he never came near John again. I sometimes get bullied by twin boys who are in my class, it's my own fault. One lad is called Myles and one Frank. The French lesson teacher Brother Alpheus (Alfie behind his back), changes pupil's names into French. Myles becomes Mealy, I never let him forget it and call him Mealy Mouth. When he objects we have a little scrap, then the bigger twin joins in. I realise then I can run faster than both of them. I now go to French lessons and learn little things like open the door, or this is a pen. I learn things on my own, so I can call a few people names without them knowing, such as you are a pig, and more. After a time learning masculine and feminine and such like things becomes a bore, I now ask Brother Alpheus if I may leave the room. Once I am in the toilets, I'm up onto the lavatory roof, climb up and walk along the high wall then drop into the street, then it's down to the docks and jump the wagons, getting loads of peanuts and brown sugar, also copra, I think it's dried coconut. If at sometime it's raining I play in a bombdy, that's a bombed house, there are lots of them about. Not once has Alfie asked why I didn't come back to class. As a result of sagging my homework suffers, so I get the brain of the class to let me copy his, on the promise of a comic of course. This fizzles out when he realises sometimes I get better marks than him, it could be that his hand writing is terrible. I have been blessed by being a good writer. He refuses to help even under threat. I still detest French. I think I'll forget my homework and settle for the strap. He's not so bad with the strap, Brother Ambrose is the worst.

THE DREADED STRAP

Brother Ambrose gave me seven belts with the strap, all in one lesson. One morning on my way to school Big Dave grabbed me and took my homework book from me, then he tore it up. Big Dave is a giant of a young man, he lives with his parents over the pawn shop in West Derby Road. He is, as my Mam says, a bit simple God love him, but as I would say he's a lot scary, he's a giant. I will give him my homework book any time he wants it,. When I went to my English lesson Brother Ambrose asked any boys who have not done their homework to come to the front of the class. I went to the front of the class and told him what had happened. "Hold your hand out boy," he shouted. "There's two for not doing your home work, don't move boy, there's another one for such a lame excuse." I had no sooner sat down, when he says come out the boys who have bad marks for their writing. I have a little smile on my face as my mate John Kelly goes out. "You boy, yes you get out here." "What for Bre?" I asked. "Put your hand out, if you had have done it you would have had poor writing." With that he gave me another two whacks with his strap, and again two more for spelling mistakes. The class have had a good laugh, but the thing that hurt me more than the strap, was the poor writing bit. I take pride in my hand writing, people always praise it. Another one I shall get my own back on when I grow up. I hate the school even more now.

We are often asked to bring in money for The Good Shepherd or towards a new school to be built sometime in the future. Some lads bring lots of money and it seems they don't get whacked all the time, these are the teacher's pets. Any coppers we do get are spent in a little shop in Grey Rock Street. It's two pence and three farthings to buy a small loaf, the two lads with a penny get the two ends with the crusts, and the lad with the three farthings gets the middle. Brother Ambrose gives me the strap again, this time for telling lies. It's Monday morning, first lesson. "Stand up and come out any boy who never went to Mass on Sunday," said he. Three boys went to the front of the class and they got whacked. Fools for owning up, I thought. "Hynes." "Yes Brother." "What colour vestments was the priest wearing?" "Were they green Brother?" I asked. "They were not boy, you didn't go, did you?" "No Brother." Two strokes for not going to Mass and two for lying. I'm definitely learning those colours I thought as I blew on my stinging hands.

WOODCOCKS CHOIR

One of our teachers is Mr Woodcock. He's not a Brother, but I reckon he is mad. He doesn't hit you with a cane or a strap, he uses a broken billiard cue. He hit me with it because I didn't have a pencil, I couldn't find one in the house. I think the girl who lives opposite borrowed it to put lines down the back of her legs to make it look like she was wearing stockings. We are told to supply our own pencils.

He tells the class the reason why he sits at his desk on one cheek, then tells us about going to bed and his wife didn't screw the top on the hot water bottle. The way he tells us is funny and he makes us laugh, then suddenly he shouts, "Joke over!" He then prowls around the class, if one boy sniggers, and it's very hard to suddenly stop, he hauls him out usually by the ear, shouting, "When I say joke over, you don't laugh any more, do you hear boy."

Mr. Woodcock doesn't take us for singing lessons, in fact nobody does, but he does make us sing in front of class, then he gives us points. You can sing any song that you know. When it's my turn I decide to sing *Beautiful Dreamer.* I only get as far as Bew!, then I hear John Kelly sniggering. I compose myself and try once more, out it comes again Bew! This time I can't compose myself, the more I try the worse it gets, followed by not just John sniggering but also most of the class. Then with a kick up my backside Woodcock tells me to sit down and I only get two points, from then on Mr Woodcock calls me Bew.

He starts a choir, calling it Woodcock's choir, telling me that I've been selected for it. I'm pretty pleased until I find that it's made up from the worst singers in the class. The song he teaches us to sing is, "Will you walk into my parlour said the spider to the fly, tis the prettiest little parlour that ever you did spy, not tonight thanks, Mr Longshanks, I've got all my fish to fry."

BOY SCOUTS

I still go to the Boy Scouts, it's the 1st Fairfield troop. Our headquarters are in the basement of The Manor House in Lark Hill Park. I mainly go because my bigger brother Jimmy is a patrol leader and he tells my Mam I have to go, that it will look bad on him if I don't. I say I'll go if I don't have to wear that big hat, its not like I can stick it in my pocket like the school cap. They win in the end and off I go, hat on and carrying a staff, being a skinny lad I feel I look like a drawing pin. I try to avoid the main roads to reach the scouts. I'm in the Tiger patrol, some scouts have arms filled with badges, woodsman badge, trackers badge. I have one badge, second class scout badge, the one everybody gets when they join. If Big Dave joined he'd more than likely get it, he'd more than likely beat me. They would make a 'destroy everybody's homework badge'. I keep going to please my Mam and older brother Jim. He is in charge of Tiger patrol and he has a ginger headed lad, his second in command. My friend Alwyn Roberts is also in Tiger patrol. I think our aim is to make life tough for our patrol leader and his deputy. We have battles with our enemy the Boys Brigade; they also wear funny hats, little round ones, much like the pageboys in American hotels.

MY BIG FEET AND ME

Still the war carries on, most lad's Dads are away fighting the enemy, either the Germans or the Japs. Nearly everything is on ration, even clothes. Some people sell their clothing coupons to the rich people so they can buy a bit more food. The other day in school I was told to go to the library, this usually means I'm in trouble because Brother Oswald, the head master, his study is in there, not this time though thank goodness. Brothers Ambrose and Brother Alpheus were in there measuring lad's feet. They had a chalk line on the floor, if the feet went over the line, the lad got extra clothing coupons. I had no chance, I only have small feet I thought. "Next boy. Ah! Little Hynes," said Brother Ambrose. "Put your heel against the wall boy." This I did, my toes were nowhere near the line. "Right boy, shuffle forward a little bit, and a bit more boy." I looked down, my toes now touched the line. "Brother Alpheus, would you say the toes touch the line or not." "Brother Ambrose, they do touch the line, I think we must have been looking at it from the wrong angle before," said the Brother. "Run along Hynes, tell your mother you'll be getting extra coupons for your big feet."

THE CUBBY HOLE

I have found another way of getting out of school early. The last lesson of the day is art, and the art teacher Brother Anastatius is old, very old. He never has a roll call so most of the class could be missing he'd never know, or care probably. To reach the art class we cross a small court yard, then up an open staircase. I make sure I'm at the back, then bunk under the stairs and into a small dark cubby hole. This is where all the cleaning stuff is kept by the caretaker. I wait pressed against the wall until it goes quiet. The library is only yards away and in it the headmaster's study. I sneak out and make my way to the lavatories, then climb up on to the wall, drop into the street and away. This worked a treat, that is until one afternoon I'd just dived into the cubby hole, then as I waited for things to go quiet I heard voices. "Well hello Frank my man, how are you getting along?" "I'm doing fine thanks Brother Oswald." Oh no! It's the head master and the caretaker. My heart sank, I was only a few feet from them. I'm suddenly terrified, what can I do? There doesn't seem to be anything I can do I thought, but wait for them to go. They didn't, they talked and talked about everything. I'm trying to keep still, it's dark in the cubby hole, and now a spider or something is crawling on my face. I'm itchy all over and I dare not move, and still they talk. I hear the class coming down the stairs and go home. In the distance I hear the screech of the trams turning the corner into Breck Road and wish I was on one, or hanging on the back. I hear the newspaper seller shouting "Last city Echo," in the street and still they talk. Then, quite suddenly, silence, they have gone. I sneak out and into the street, running to catch the tram and get home before my Mam. No chance, my Mam is waiting. "Come here you, where have you been until now?" "In school Mam, honest." I wasn't telling lies, but I won't be doing that again. Anyway, I like art and I'm pretty good at it. My Dad paints in oils when he's on leave, he mixes his paints on the lid of a tobacco tin. He must have been in love with Ginger Rogers, paintings of her are on a few panels of our doors at home. He couldn't afford canvas to paint on more than likely.

COCK OF THE CLASS

I'm in trouble again in school, because I wont tell Brother Ambrose what Eddy Doran was doing to make me laugh. He had the desk lid up, and was smacking his boy hood with the ruler, silly but true. I wouldn't snitch off him because I'm sure the Brother knew, and secondly Eddy was the cock of the class, in more ways than one. I didn't want a belt off him. Every school day at four o'clock Brother Ambrose would ask the same question, "What was Doran doing to make you laugh?" Every day I would reply, "Nothing Brother." Over to Brother Oswald's study I would go. It is in a room within the library. It has a massive big oak door. I tap gently on it, hoping he doesn't hear. From his study I hear him singing, always the same song, "Come back Paddy Riley, from over the sea, come back Paddy Riley to me." I knock a bit louder now, either I'm getting braver or I'm sick of Paddy Riley. The door opens, a huge black form is at the door, it's Brother Oswald. "Hah! Little Hynes," he booms. "Come in, come in, what have you been doing now? Why, can't you be like your big brother?" I think, just beat me up, I hate being compared to my older brother, and you go and find Paddy Riley wherever he is, and bring him back. Brother Oswald keeps me behind each night for ages, but I still won't tell him. In the end I decide I can't hold out much longer, but now I have a problem, I don't know how to describe it to the Brother. "Err! He was playing with his mickey Brother Oswald," I blurted out. "Oh his private," said the Brother. "You may go now."

TAKING THE MICKS

I now wish to keep pigeons, so I'm making a pigeon loft on top of the air raid shelter. If we get bombed the micks will go first. A boy in school, John Harris, his Dad has given me a pair of young birds, these are called squeakers, and must be the ugliest looking things ever. We also catch a few pigeons in town. There is also a big deserted house in Norris Green Park, it's ancient, only at the very top are there any rafters left. By climbing along the wall that adjoins the house, it starts off low then gets higher and higher until it's level with the roof, we climb in, and lots of pigeons roost there. Shining a torch into their faces, they don't move, then we pick out the ones that are only young. Last week we were balanced on the rafters and the park policeman came, he knew we were up in the rafters so we kept very quiet. He was shining his torch to try to see us, he was about to give up when one of the lads trumped, then the giggling started, then more trumping. The more you tried to stop giggling the worse it got. The parky was fuming, he said he was waiting for us to come down, and what he wouldn't do to us. He was still shouting as we quietly crawled along the wall and out of the park.

My Mam isn't keen at all on me keeping pigeons, she reckons that they bring bad luck if they land on your roof, so I soap their wings, and throw them on to Mrs Durkin's roof. Then I coax them back down with some corn, unknowingly supplied by Mrs Harper's corn store. I'm so keen to toss them that I find a cardboard box and pack them in. I manage to get on the tram with them. I'm on my way to school so I get off a stop early, at the junction of West Derby Road and Belmont Road, opposite St. Margaret's Church, and then as the pigeon fanciers say, I toss them. Actually all you do is throw them in the air. After standing and watching them a couple almost hitting the overhead tram wires, I make my way to school. School drags today, I can't wait to see my pigeons at home and settled on their perches. I'm in luck, the last lesson is French, after the usual "May I leave the room Brother?", I'm off home. Leaping off the tram I ran like the devil was after me straight to the loft. Empty, not a feather never mind a pigeon. I'm so disappointed. I'm still looking in the sky for any sign of them when my Mam comes home. "What are you looking for son? I don't think there are any German planes up there tonight, there hasn't been any for ages." Then I told her what had happened. "What time was this, did you say on your way to school? Oh! Give up lad they could of walked home by now." That's ended my dream of becoming a pigeon fancier. Each time I pass the church now I look up and wonder if my pigeons are up there flying around the steeple. My Mam was right though about them being unlucky, the church burnt down.

ALDER HEY HOSPITAL

I'm beginning to feel sick lately. I still go to school, although some days I can't keep my eyes open, I can't pay attention to what the teacher is saying. No one seems to know that I'm ill. At the Scouts we have boxing. I'm matched against Alwyn Roberts who I can beat any time, but tonight he battered me. Even my younger brother beats me over our usual battle of the bed clothes. "He only wants to stay off school, or he wants to get off his share of going on the messages," is all I hear. At last my Mam is taking me to hospital, after weeks of no-one believing me that I feel ill. We are walking along the stile, Meadow Lane to West Derby Village, it's cold as the wind is blowing in our faces, and it's a bad winters day. After a long time because it is a Sunday service, the bus arrives. When we reach the hospital, the nurses wrap me in a red blanket and rush me to a ward. I don't remember any more except hearing some one saying he's a very sick boy, and that I have acute rheumatic fever. I have been sleeping a lot, and the thought of not having to go on the milk round of a morning or sharing my bed with my brother, which usually finishes up with a fight over the bed clothes or the overcoat, makes me feel better. Feeling better didn't last long. I've caught mumps and I'm in a ward on my own, no one is allowed in, only the nurse and she wears a mask. My Mam and Dad I see looking through a window, my Dad must be on leave.

After a couple of weeks I'm now back on the main ward, and feeling much better. There are lots of wounded soldiers in the hospital, they wear light blue suits, and all the top wards are theirs. I have been in hospital a couple of months now, my Mam can't get to see me very often. It's late when she gets home from work, she then has to feed the kids. The lad in the next bed is the same, his Mam can't get here very much. He's now become my mate his name is John, he lives in Atholl Street which is next to the street my Aunty Molly lives in. When it's visiting time we put on our sad faces, the one my Mam says will get me the Parish. Somebody's Mam always comes over with a few sweets or fruit. I feel a bit guilty at times, because we seem to finish up with more stuff than the rest of the ward. Although there hasn't been any air raids lately, we still have a blackout, of a night there is only one light and it has red paper wrapped around it to dim it. John and I take advantage of this and get up to all kinds. When my Mam does come in Sister Owen tells her that I won't stay in bed, "It's his heart not mine, he must stay in bed Mrs Hynes." My Mam as usual says, "Have you been making a show of me again? I don't know what I'll do with you lad."

VANTAS AND A KISS

We have a lovely nurse, her name is nurse Finnessy. We call her Finny, she told us we must call her Finny. She is usually with a soldier in the kitchen when it's lights out. John and I then serenade her with a song we made up, it goes "Someone's in the kitchen with Finny, someone's in the kitchen we know, someone's in the kitchen with Finny, and she's playing on his old banjo." She tries to tell us off, but I can see her smiling. After this, each night to settle the ward down, Finny gives every one a drink of lemonade and a goodnight kiss. I'm in the end bed when Nurse Finny says "Oh dear, I've run out of lemonade, will you have Vantas, it's nice." After a short time, she's back from the kitchen with a glass of Vantas. I took a swig of the Vantas and spat it out all over everywhere. "That's horrible," I gasped. "You don't know what's good for you," said nurse Finny, who took a sip and was violently sick. Then it clicked - a few weeks ago a nurse couldn't be bothered getting John and I a bottle, so we piddled in a bottle. The next morning we played rolling it to each other along the wooden floor. A nurse confiscated it, it was a brown Vantas bottle. No way would I tell Finny that.

The weeks go by, very slowly. I still don't get any visitors apart from my Mam when she can get in, but today I have two visitors, Brothers Ambrose and Alpheus, who are standing rather sheepishly at the foot of my bed. Brother Ambrose tosses a few comics and some sweets on the bed, "We confiscated these from the boys," he said. They don't hate me after all, I think. First they fiddled some clothing coupons for my Mam by turning my feet from a size five to a ten, now they have given me these presents. Miracles do happen. After a bit of a strained conversation and a few prayers for me, they have left. When I told my Mam about their prayers, she said the prayers were more likely for the nursing staff, God help them for having to put up with me.

IN THE WEE SMALL HOURS

My friend and I have a new game to pass the time away. The edges of the blankets are bound with twine, we pick it off. Then when a nurse comes with the trolley, we manage to get a few swab sticks. If you bend one gently and tie twine on it, then it becomes a little bow. The other sticks are our arrows. We have lots of fun with these until we discover a bottle of Swan ink, dip the swabs in it, and splatter a few nice white counter panes. Now everything is confiscated. John and I behave ourselves for the next few weeks, but a boy is now in our ward, a big fat boy who looks like he's old enough to be in a grown ups hospital. He is always bullying the other lads, he mocks the little kids who wet their beds, so John and I decided to teach him a lesson. All evening we didn't go for a wee or use a bottle, we were in agony waiting for him to go to sleep. After checking many times he fell asleep, on tip toes and very quietly John and I crept across the ward. Only one dim light was on and that had red paper covering it. Gently peeling his blanket back, John and I wee'd and wee'd in his bed, making sure to be awake early in the morning when the Sister came around with the Matron. "A big boy like you," the Matron was saying, and the lad was going all colours. He won't be making fun at any more little kids, ever again.

WAR IS OVER

My Mam visits me, saying the Germans are on the run, and the war could soon be over. There is a buzz about the hospital, the wounded soldiers seem to be more cheerful and the staff. Then one day I saw lots of people kissing and dancing. It was over, Germany has surrended. We're having a party, Sister Owen has made trifle, it's vile, and she tells me if I don't eat it there will be nothing else for me. Sometimes it pays to be next to the sluice, I just hope it doesn't block the sewers in the hospital. My mother has been told that she can take me home shortly. The day arrives for me to go home. My Mam has brought a Macintosh for me to go home in, it's massive. She asks the nurses if it's too big on me, I can feel her pulling it in at the back. I was that keen to get out of hospital I would have gone home wearing a tent. My

Mam sold it later to a neighbour, it was big on him and he was about six feet tall. I found a little kitten before I went in hospital, it had a rope around its neck and had been mistreated. Every

time my Mam visited me I'd ask was the kitten any bigger, no, no she would say, and there it is, as big as a tiger. She gave my rabbits away, all but the big Flemish Giant. There was no one to look after them, she said, so I give them to Mr Fletcher. His son keeps rabbits, she said. "Mam, Mr Fletcher is a butcher, he owns a shop." "I know lad, but his son keeps them as pets." "Yes Mam, and I bet he keeps lambs and cattle and hangs them up in his Dad's shop."

WELCOME HOME CHARLIE

Troop ships are docking at the landing stage at the Pier Head bringing service men and women home from the war to be demobbed and to be united again with their families. There are lots of parties taking place. Some that arrive home have been prisoners of war. Some lads have fun by altering the welcome home signs, 'Welcome Home Our Charlie, three years a P.O.W.' now reads, 'Welcome Home Our Charlie, three years in the Potato Queue'. The war with Japan carries on, Mrs Harrison is in our house for her usual cup of cocoa and a chinwag with my Mam. "I wonder how our poor Georgie is getting along with them little yellow b-------s Annie," then says, "Anderem, I went over on the ferry to see my sister in Birkenhead, they're snooty tuppence ha'penny toffs over there. I went in to the market and asked this one for half a pound of pigs belly. Looking down her nose at me, she said "Do you mean Hodge?" "Anderem," I said, " I don't care what its name was, just give me half a pound."

I'm soon back running around with my mates, still catching the ferry across the river. On one of our walks across Arrowe Park, we have come across hundreds of tanks, they are being stored in a compound. They have served their usefulness and must be awaiting their fate, no-one seems to be guarding them, so under the fence we go. It's a dream come true for us lads, as in and out of them we climb, inside everything that has been left, goggles, maps, gloves, and even bullets. After pretending to fire and kill about a thousand German soldiers each, we make our way home, war torn but happy.

OPEN AIR SCHOOL

My Mam has told me that I won't be going back to St. Elizabeth's, instead I will be attending Margaret Beavan Open Air School. This is in Almonds Green, near West Derby Village. After a few weeks of resting or supposed to be, I start in school. I dreaded going, lots of kids call it the soft school. Boys and girls who have been ill attend the school, kids who have had T.B. or as in my case Rheumatic Fever, and other illnesses, such as Epilepsy. One lad lights a cigarette stump up in class and Mr Coglan tells us to leave him, then the lad comes out of his fit and carries on as normal. Other lads have fits, kicking and twisting on the floor, my bad luck is starting in the middle of a term, not knowing anybody. The school bully and his little gang start picking on me, he calls himself O'iorns. I hate him, I sneaked a look in the register and his name is spelt O'nions. I then take delight in calling him Onions. One day going into the toilets I bumped into him, "Hiya Onions," I said. "Are you going for a leek?" He went all colours, he was furious. He wants to fight me in the lavatories. I'm scared, but my Mam taught me never to back down to a bully. When I had a fight on the field, when I was in the juniors in Monksdown Road, a lady split us up, she battered us with her shopping bag, shouting "There's enough fighting going on in the world without you two." I was glad really, I was getting beat, but this is a funny fight. When he's on top and winning, it carries on for ages, but when I'm on top his mates jump in shouting end of the round, he doesn't come near me again, and over time I make my own mates. It's a lot different than St. Lizzies, the teachers are not allowed to cane you, the pupils have a canvas bed which folds up when not in use to lie on after dinner, the dinners are nice, and to me, after my last school, this is great.

JAPAN SURRENDERS

The Americans have dropped a couple of massive bombs on Japan, and the Japanese forces have surrended. Mrs. Harrison will get her son George back, people are lighting bonfires again and having parties. Food is still rationed and it's reckoned it will be for a long time. Some of the dads are now being demobbed from the forces, and there's lots of lads who are not too happy, they haven't seen their dads for the best part of six years, and suddenly a man is in the house telling them what to do. Their Mams have fed and looked after them for six years, lads have grown up in those years. We've grown a bit now, talking to girls instead of tying them to the lamppost or sitting behind them in the pictures and without them knowing tying their long hair together.

In Storrington Avenue a little dance, in what was a Nissan hut, has started up. A few records are played, a lad turns the handle on the gramophone, this is balanced on a chair. A few girls we know from our street go there and ask us to meet them, we turn up and don't feel a bit comfortable. The boys who run the dance are from the posh houses and fancy the girls, so won't let us join. They let the girls join and we get asked to leave, or as Bobby said, "We've been chucked out." It's a cold night and we see the smoke curling out of the chimney and into the night air. We all seem to think as one, what if we block the chimney, it's only a stove with a tin chimney. Up on to the roof we climbed. Other mates threw some sods of grass up, these we stuck on top of the chimney. We climbed down and hid. First it was one window opening, then two, then lots. The doors burst open. We felt rather pleased, the dance was called off, and we walked the girls home. They said it was too full of smoke to stay. "You didn't have anything to do with that tonight?" asked one of the girls. "No it was some sods that we know," said Bobby with an innocent face. Weeks have gone by and they still wont let us join.

Paddy O'Hanlon keeps his horse tied to a rope in the field, it's not very big, it's more of a pony. We decide that tonight it's going to the dance. Quietly we untie the rope, then lead it to the doors. They are double doors with push bars like ones that are fitted on church hall doors, a good push and they fly open. A smack on the pony's bum and it was in. I've heard of a fox trot dance, this was a pony trot, scattering chairs plus the gramophone. It stopped short of the stage, and then it began plopping as it trotted around the dance floor. I expected Sid to run in with his little cart, and shovel it up for his Dad's rhubarb. Now we know we'll never be allowed in. Then again, who wants to go to a dance with such a filthy floor.

AN APPLE FOR THE TEACHER

I like going to my new school, the lessons are a lot easier than the ones in St. Lizzies. The things I was taught in St. Lizzies put me near the top of the class here, never top. Some lads are so badly crippled they use their brains a lot more. We have gardening as a lesson, raking and hoeing the vegetables which are growing in the orchard. Mr. Coglan is our teacher, he is a nice man, just out of the army, he was a captain. But today he's Mr. Angry. When his back was turned both Gerry Callaghan and myself hurled our rakes into the apple tree. This usually rewards us with a few apples, but not today. Gerry's rake came back down to earth, but mine decided to stay up the tree. "Hynes." "Yes sir." "Where's your rake?" I was about to make up a story when the rake fell upon Mr Coglan's head. "Ouch!" he yelled. "Six years in the army and not a mark, here I am in the safety of an English garden, with a cut head. Two hundred lines lad, 'I must use the garden rake for the purpose it was intended', and I want them by tomorrow." "Thank you sir, sorry sir," is all I could mutter, thinking how lucky I am that it isn't St. Lizzies, and it's not Brother Ambrose.

FOOTBALL AND CRICKET

Despite some early set backs with Mr. Coglan, I like him, he's a fair man, he also does not like spoilt brats. One of these is a lad named Robert Gibbons. I'm pleased when he tells him off for putting Bobby Gibbons on his exercise book, "Your name is Robert, not Bobby, change it," said Mr Coglan. The reason I think Gibbons is a brat is because he's in our Scouts. We went camping to Tawd Vale, which is near Ormskirk. I helped to pull the trek cart all the way home. He having to wear a built up boot sat on the top all the way home, he had a rope and was cracking it like a whip, while shouting Mush! When I asked if I could have a rest up there because my foot was hurting, he wouldn't get down. On reaching home my Mam put my foot under the cold water tap, then cut my boot off. I had walked home with a sprained ankle.

I'm now the school captain. One of my jobs is to run after and bring back a lad who is always running away. Each time Mr Coglan tells him off he's up and away. "Hynes go and bring him back." I usually catch him near West Derby village. I'm pretty pleased about being the school captain, mainly because I'm given the keys to the wash rooms and cloak rooms, to make sure no lads stay in them. I lock them up, but have a little skive myself.

One thing I'm not to do in school is to play sport, this meaning football and other games. We secretly play football on the far playground away from the teachers, it's usually the Hearts v the Rest. It sounds like a Scottish football match, but it's all boys with heart conditions versus the rest of the boys. Even though Mr Coglan tells the class when picking a team, don't pick Hynes, I still get selected. Mr Coglan relents, he says I can bat in cricket, as long as someone runs for me, and play football only if I'm in goal. Bowling and fielding I'm okay, but batting hopeless, this is found out in our first match. I'm out first ball, just as well I thought, looking at my runner he has an iron on his leg. Football is no better, we get beat eight nil, I'm the goalie. I'm not asked again. I'm still suffering with a bad back, with picking the ball out of the net.

Things outside of school are still the same, food still rationed and a coal shortage. My Dad is demobbed, and looking for work. My Mam doesn't work in the café any more, she told my Dad there are jobs in the postal service. He told her he does not want to wear a uniform again, whether it be a postman or a tram conductor. He gets a job as a boiler man in the recruiting centre in Pall Mall Square. My Mam wants to brighten the house up a bit with some new furniture. My Dad won't sign any form to get it on the never, never. "You can sign for it son," she tells me. "You write just like him, he'd be content to sit on an old orange box." I left school last week and had an interview in Saxone Buildings in Church Street. It was for an apprentice buyer for a gold and jewellery merchants, I had to take my Mam with me, I passed the interview, but they wanted both parents to sign a form. It stated on it if I lost or stole any article they would make good the loss. My Dad wouldn't sign, and I can't sign myself, as he would know when I started the job, so next week instead I begin work along the canal in a wood mill. Never mind, I'm still here. If our boys hadn't won the Battle Of Britain we would have more than likely have been put against a wall and shot, or worse, still forced to work pea picking, without pay. My elder brother James has been called up to do his National service, he's going to Germany with the Kings Regiment. Seems like it was only yesterday he was a boy peeping out of the air raid shelter, to see if he recognised any German planes, and rationing still goes on.

THE END